Herbert John (Tom) Thompson

Governance as Stewardship

An Exploration of the Relationship Between the Practice of Shared Leadership and Board Effectiveness

LAP LAMBERT Academic Publishing

Impressum / Imprint

Bibliografische Information der Deutschen Nationalbibliothek: Die Deutsche Nationalbibliothek verzeichnet diese Publikation in der Deutschen Nationalbibliografie; detaillierte bibliografische Daten sind im Internet über http://dnb.d-nb.de abrufbar.

Bibliographic information published by the Deutsche Nationalbibliothek: The Deutsche Nationalbibliothek lists this publication in the Deutsche Nationalbibliografie; detailed bibliographic data are available in the Internet at http://dnb.d-nb.de.

Coverbild / Cover image: www.ingimage.com

Verlag / Publisher:
LAP LAMBERT Academic Publishing
ist ein Imprint der / is a trademark of
OmniScriptum GmbH & Co. KG
Heinrich-Böcking-Str. 6-8, 66121 Saarbrücken, Deutschland / Germany
Email: info@lap-publishing.com

Herstellung: siehe letzte Seite /
Printed at: see last page
ISBN: 978-3-659-76891-0

ACKNOWLEDGEMENTS

I thank the presidents, chairpersons, executive assistants, and board members who participated in this study for their time and their candidness. Their stories and support provided rich insights into shared leadership and the role of the board in a governance sense in shaping institutional direction and performance.

I wish to extend my sincere gratitude to my advisor, Dr. David Kirby. His wise counsel and the rigor he expected in the preparation of the thesis contributed greatly to the quality and caliber of this work. I thank him, as well, for his understanding, encouragement, patience and sense of humor when the 'going got tough.' My dedication and capacity to complete this exploration were greatly directed and supported by his involvement and the scholarship which he brought to the project.

I also wish to thank committee members Dr. Devon Jensen and Dr. Colleen Kawalilak, who were understanding and inspirational throughout the journey and provided me with countless insightful suggestions. In addition, I wish to thank Dr. Claudia Emes and Dr. Paula Brook for their perspicacity, respect, and wisdom in examining my dissertation.

I wish to extend my sincere gratitude to two special friends and colleagues, Dr. Abimbola Abiola and Paulette Shoemaker. Dr. Abiola was a wonderful mentor and statistical guru throughout this work. He provided much-needed and timely expertise in the analyzing of the data and presentation of the results of my work. Similarly, Paulette Shoemaker was instrumental in shaping the final dissertation with her considerable skills in editing, formatting, and word processing.

The completion of a doctorate of education affects not only those engaged in the study but their families and friends as well. To all who encouraged and sustained my efforts, thank you.

DEDICATION

This work is dedicated to my wife and my very best friend, Joyce. Your continual love, wisdom, commitment and support sustained me throughout the thesis process and in my life. I feel truly blessed that you chose to share your life with me as your partner. I love you. Thank you.

TABLE OF CONTENTS

LIST OF TABLES

LIST OF FIGURES AND ILLUSTRATIONS

CHAPTER 1

INTRODUCTION

This chapter provides the background and purpose(s) of the inquiry and presents the problem statement and research questions that guide the study. As well, this chapter demonstrates the significance of the study and outlines the operative definitions, assumptions, delimitations, and limitations within the inquiry.

Background of the Researcher

The researcher has worked in the Alberta public higher education sector for over 20 years as an instructor, chairperson, vice-president and president. During my tenure as president of two rural, public colleges, I have drawn upon a diverse background in education, governance, coaching, marketing and management. In my capacity as president and chief executive officer, I work with government, industry, and communities to achieve a Community Learning Campus goal of a seamless and integrated learning environment, one which will assist students, specifically, who wish to remain and study in rural Western Canada.

I am a strong supporter of the Association of Canadian Community Colleges, where I have held positions on the Association's Executive and Board of Directors. As well, I serve as one of two Canadian members on the leadership team of the North American Rural Colleges and Communities Alliance. Other governance-related roles have included Chairperson of the Alberta Association of Colleges and Technical Institutes, Founding Vice-Chairperson of eCampus Alberta and the Canadian representative to the UNESCO Conference on Re-engineering Technical Vocational Education in China.

Background to the Study

It is fair to say that nonprofit governance in Western Canadian rural, public colleges is acknowledged as important. The effectiveness with which boards exercise their authority may have considerable influence on the provision of higher education in their institution. However, what appears to be less understood is how to maximize the collective capacity towards improving board effectiveness.

In a time of institutional accountability and with a provincial hue and cry for better governance, there does not appear to be a corresponding body of social research emerging and articulating a compelling case for governance reform. Recently, even at the provincial level, David Swann (2006), Member of the Legislative Assembly for Calgary Mountain View, outlined his governance-related concerns and frustrations in a member's statement during the spring sitting when he stated, "this government has failed to deliver the three most fundamental elements of governance – a vision grounded in a framework, a scientific assessment of present and projected impacts, and the development of meaningful public involvement in decision-making."

2

With the absence of a decision-making framework, higher education officials are besieged with countless epistemologies of leadership and, to a significantly lesser degree, various attempts by unions and associations to persuade academic organizations of the virtues of shared governance. Likewise, organizational theorists continue to weigh in and recommend shared decision-making as a key strategy in the improvement of performance in organizations.

In fact, Barnes and Noble (2004) listed 27,220 books with the word "leader" or "leadership", compared to 2,349 with the keyword "trustee", "trusteeship", or "governance".

Historically, university faculty and staff have claimed that shared decision-making is vital in the maintenance of the academic integrity of the institution. In the Canadian Association of University Teachers (CAUT) Discussion Paper, *The CAUT Policy on Governance – Where we have been and where we should go,* the Association outlined their policy [currently under review] relative to university governance. CAUT policy states that, "effective governance requires that faculty members and librarians, given their professional competence, should be involved at the highest levels...At the same time, effective governance presupposes that the various constituencies in the university – faculty and librarians, support staff, and students have effective associations or unions to represent their interests" (p. 70). Shared decision-making, as noted by the American Federation of Teachers (2006), is seen in this context to be integral in the prevention of institutional commercialization and the possible distortion of the institution's educational mission, or the erosion of the quality, academic freedom, and collegiality.

At an intuitive level, there appears to be an emerging school of thought towards the notion that the governance process is much more than policy-making, strategic and business plan approvals, operational and capital budgets monitoring, and the overseeing of ever-dynamic organizational structures. However, some times the governance process can be dismissed by leadership traditionalists as marginally relevant, somewhat inert, time-consuming, or only somewhat mission critical to the institution's well-being.

In speaking to the relevance issue, David Kilgour (1999), the former federal Liberal Member of Parliament for Edmonton-Beaumont, in his remarks to the 1999 Laurentian Seminar on Parliament and the Challenge of Good Governance, cited *Searching for Good Governance* (1994), the final report of the Government and Competitiveness Project, by Bryne Purchase and Ronald Hirschhorn. He offered:

> On the premise that governance matters [to competitiveness], the report identified eight basic principles for the design of good governance that should form the basis for making necessary institutional changes. These principles were as follows: focus on outputs, make decisions transparent, provide incentives, establish constraints, promote competition, link costs and benefits, encourage commitment and loyalty, and maintain trust through fairness (p. 33).

Consistent with the aforementioned report, it would appear that the world's complexities and challenges call for a broader worldview of governance at the institutional level. Underscoring the work of Peters and Waterman (1982), it would seem an understanding is necessary and that organizational effectiveness has become much more a function of wisdom not necessarily intellect, being brilliant not dismissive on the basics, thinking as opposed to the accumulation of tools, and constantly adhering to the need to simplify things. Today's high performing institutions appear to apply persistence and insist on quality, service, and excellence. Jack Welch (2005), General Electric's 8th Chairman and CEO, encourages institutions, when considering major reforms, to "bring out the three old warhorses of competition – quality, service, [and cost] – and drive them to new levels (p. 342). High performing institutions appear to stress the importance of placing the client at the centre of their planning and implementation and appear to treat their staff, and partners with dignity and respect. Tom Peters (1997) contended that over the next 10 to 15 years the primary strategic battle, in virtually any industry you can name, will be the battle to see who can go the furthest in empowering employees (p. 253). They seem to promote mistake-making, without penalty, and celebrate their champions, while maintaining a high tolerance for ambiguity in a highly experimental workplace. R.W. Johnson, Jr., former CEO, 3M Corporation, in Collins and Porras's (1994), *Built to Last*, once said that "failure is our most important product" (p. 140).

Consequently, the long-standing notion(s) that the high performing institution is a function of a smooth and effective bureaucracy run by a talented CEO appears to be questionable and its basic tenants seem to be more nuanced at the present. Relative to higher education, colleges have changed more in the past 10 years than in the previous 40. As noted by Bolman and Deal (1997), mind boggling advances in technology, globalism, and significantly shortened product and service life cycles have produced a need for more flexible, adaptable, and fluid organizational forms (p. 9).

Hence, the time may have arrived, as purported by Chait, Ryan and Taylor (2005) to attempt to understand governance, not just do governance, as it would seem obvious that effective institutional governing necessitates much more than bright people using common sense and doing what comes naturally.

From an Alberta perspective, this timing aligns well with the release of the final report, *A Learning Alberta* (2006), from the steering committee who was charged with the responsibility of consultation and providing recommendations in addressing the key issues facing the advanced learning system over the next 20 years. These issues include the access and inspiring of learning in populations that are currently under-represented, particularly in rural, remote, and northern areas of the province and could be served by rural, public colleges.

Lastly, understanding higher education governance in a rural, remote, or northern context may fit into what social scientists call a new paradigm, within which it becomes a part of a larger rural-based mosaic that includes interrelated institutions such as community, partnerships, organizations, and industry. Jean (2004), the Canada Research Chair in Rural Development, in his essay, *The Road to Successful Rural Community Development: Ten Winning Conditions*, found in the National Rural Economy [NRE], suggested that the advent of a new rural governance model has arrived and it is defined as a "breaking-out" by communities [colleges] from the traditional areas of jurisdiction imposed upon them by higher levels of government. Thus, the new rural governance model designates this innovative approach to exercising power and making decisions, and it involves three broad categories of forces. They are as follows: (1) the municipal power, (2) the power of private economic entities with local operations, and (3) the power of integrated community organizations.

Therefore, one of the primary differentiations between rural and urban board governance in the public Western Canadian college sector may be the growing autonomy of the rural colleges away from doing governance and their leadership towards the prudent management of community relationships and the proper leveraging of the college's social and economic capital. Jean (2004) asserted that the new way that communities, or boards, have found to organize their decision-making for the socio-economic life and good of the community, or institution, is centered in "capacity-building" meaning the ability to manage their own affairs effectively and efficiently (p. 62).

Purpose of the Study

The purpose of this study was to explore the relationship between the practice of shared leadership and board effectiveness within the boards of the rural, public colleges. In order to achieve the purpose of improving board effectiveness, the study sought to identify and interpret changes in the way a board thinks and works collectively due to four governance factors. As suggested in the literature, they are as follows: (1) president's competency and

7

performance, (2) human capital of the board, (3) education and training, and (4) stewardship and the college's voice. This included describing the concept of shared leadership, defining and describing the four factors of improving board effectiveness, and analyzing changes in the way boards think and work collectively through an analytical framework of specific behavior(s) theory, based primarily upon the work developed by Chait, Holland, and Taylor (1996). This framework delineated six competency sets inherent in effective boards. The goal of the study was to identify board effectiveness patterns and themes, as a function of the practice of shared leadership, which may assist in explaining the effects on institutional performance.

Research Design

This was a mixed method research study primarily from an epistemology of objectivism. The integrated approach adopted for this study utilized the interpretive methodology of survey research using an ethnographic questionnaire, which was informed by the semi-structured interview method(s) of research, followed by statistical analysis. The integrated approach was intended to facilitate the development of a holistic worldview of the improvement of board effectiveness, as a function of practicing shared leadership, and how this may affect institutional performance. The intentions of the study were operationalized in the statement of the problem and research questions which follow.

8

Statement of the Problem

The frustration with nonprofit boards and board members in the higher education sector is not necessarily about inexperience or confusion about roles and responsibility. The bigger issue which appears to loom behind these problems of effectiveness is more fundamental in nature. Specifically, the issue appears to be about the degree to which a board embraces and engages in the practice of shared leadership. Therefore, it was useful to assess the practice(s) of shared leadership by a rural public college board of governors and its impact upon their board governance effectiveness.

Research Questions

Consistent with the purpose and problem statement, the following five research questions were used to guide this exploration:

1. To what extent do board members in rural, public colleges understand the eight concepts of shared leadership and board governance effectiveness, as noted in the literature by Smith (2001)?
2. To what extent do boards of rural, public colleges practice the six characteristics of shared leadership, as outlined in the literature by Nemerowicz and Rosi (1997)?
3. To what extent does the institution's performance, as quantified in the literature by Alberta Advanced Education (2006), reflect the degree of shared leadership practiced by the board of a rural, public college?
4. What is the extent of the contribution of each of the four governance factors, as identified in the literature, towards board effectiveness?

9

5. To what extent does the rural community's commitment and capacity to learn reflect its college board's proficiency to work in all three governance as leadership modes, as noted in the literature by Chait (2005)?

Significance of the Study

From a governance perspective, the primary significance of this social research was based in the notion that there is a relationship between the practice of shared leadership and board effectiveness. As well, this relationship may indeed contribute to a change in an institution's performance. It was anticipated that this investigation may impact on the way higher education officials, in Western Canada, choose to understand rather than do governance. Likewise, as a result of this study, one may anticipate higher education officials taking a more critical look at recruitment, appointment, and the orientation practices associated with new board members. For instance, it is anticipated this study may play a role in the program planning and design of governance education and training for new and ongoing board members. In short, the better higher education officials understand the relationship between effective board governance and the concept of shared leadership, in a rural context, the better the chance of the boards understanding their higher purpose of governance. Furthermore, the better the board understands their governance purpose, the better governed may be their institution, which, in turn, may influence improved institutional performance.

Definition of Terms

The following words or phrases are presented as operative definitions to facilitate the communication of the material within this study.

The Public College and Technical Institute System

There are 17 colleges and technical public institutions in the Alberta Public College and Technical Institute System. Within the 17 institutions, there are nine non-metro, or rural, public colleges – Grande Prairie Regional College, Keyano College, Portage College, Northern Lakes College, Lakeland College, Red Deer College, Olds College, Lethbridge Community College and Medicine Hat College.

Shared Leadership

It is the governance act, in concert with the administration, of a board facilitating the development of the institution's vision, the determining of the preferred future state, and ensuring the resources are in place to effectively achieve the same.

Institutional Performance

Performance is measured by five components, which are assessed annually and articulated by the Ministry of Advanced Education and Technology, within the Ministry's performance envelope: (1) strategic and ongoing enrolment growth, (2) efficient financial management and performance, (3) demonstrated enterprise revenue development, (4) student satisfaction, and (5) employer satisfaction.

Board Governance Effectiveness

Effectiveness is evidenced in the board's knowledge, skill, and ability to steward on a consistent basis the institution's values, vision, mission, and ends. They do so by understanding and exhibiting their four primary roles and responsibilities – fiduciary, policy development, monitoring of performance, and the development of two-way external relations linkages.

Policy Boards

They are characteristic of larger organizations and institutions with highly qualified chief executive officers and professional administrations. They are primarily concerned with governance, strategic planning, and reviewing reports and recommendations from their senior administration and their standing committees. Their orientation is primarily focused on policy development, while taking an external and long-term view. The policy board in the public, nonprofit sector is the closest in function to the corporate board in the for-profit private sector.

Public [Nonprofit] Boards

They govern institutions chartered to serve governmental and charitable interests. Their main responsibility is to build and maintain an effective organization within the charter's [legislative] purpose. There is no stock ownership and therefore no distribution of profits. Any surpluses must be recapitalized. These institutions receive a large proportion of revenue from funding, enterprise revenue(s), and donations rather than from the sales of products or taxation.

Assumptions, Delimitations and Limitations

Assumptions

Based on the parameters of this study, the following are assumed:

1. As a result of methodological and epistemological procedures, the researcher did not introduce a bias to the study that may have influenced the results.

2. The timing of the study did not have a significant effect on the results.

3. Individual respondents provided data that was authentic, honest, and accurate.

4. The respondent's perceptions of the meaning intended by research instruments and all inquiry communication were accurate.

5. The survey questions were sufficiently comprehensive, reliable and valid to describe the effects on board effectiveness and institutional performance by rural, public college boards, which practiced shared leadership.

6. The research developed a basic understanding of shared leadership within a governance context, which included how individual board members, presidents, and board chairpersons perceived the concept.

7. The documents, which were analyzed, were relevant and current in defining the impact of shared leadership.

Delimitations

This study was delimited to an analysis of data collected utilizing field methods, which included the review and analysis of institutional and board documents. Working with the board secretaries the data were collected, which included artifacts such as government documents pertaining to performance envelope awards, and institutional documents pertaining to annual reports, presidential search, board orientation manuals, board policy manuals, board approved business plans, and professional development workshops agendas, along with supporting materials. The purpose was to achieve theoretical soundness and to narrow the focus to eight Western Canadian rural, public colleges, which formed the basis for surveying each member of the institution's boards. The generalizability of the study was further delimited by the composition of the selected subject(s) sample population, with eight rural, public colleges selected from within one Western Canadian province. Lastly, only board chairpersons and presidents were selected for the semi-structured interview sample population.

Limitations

Having given careful thought to problems involving ethics and feasibility, it is noted that inherent and limiting conditions arose within the study, including a small sample size, the use of a limited number of techniques for gathering data and selection procedures (Rossman & Rallis, 1998). As well, the fact that the researcher is a member of the proposed subject sample population and possessed in-depth knowledge of the Western Canadian rural, public colleges should be taken into consideration. However, having considered that the information to be gained from the compromised aspects of the study may be nevertheless valid and useful, this researcher proposed to proceed having duly noted the restrictive weaknesses.

Additionally, due to the fact that the unit of analysis was delimited to eight Western Canadian rural, public colleges, including their respective board chairpersons and presidents, the researcher's findings may not be safely generalizable beyond this subject sample population. Furthermore, the findings may only reflect the assumptions of these specific higher education officials during the time period March 2007 through May 2007. Furthermore, it is noted that the findings may have been further limited due to the respondents to the survey and semi-structured interviewees not fully understanding the issues associated with shared leadership and its effect on the performance of their institution.

CHAPTER 2

LITERATURE REVIEW

Within a context of nonprofit organizational governance and aligned with the statement of the problem and research questions the following literature review is designed to introduce six sets of literature relevant to the study of board effectiveness and shared leadership. To provide a review of the nonprofit organization literature related to governance, the Introduction, or the first set, is divided into 10 sections. They are as follows:

1. Background
2. What is a Nonprofit Organization?
3. Increased Demand for Good Governance
4. Governance and Stakeholders
5. Knowledge about Governance
6. Recruitment and Diversity
7. A Competent CEO
8. Accountability, Transparency and Stewardship
9. Measuring Board Effectiveness
10. Major Themes

Following the Introduction, the researcher focuses on the board governance effectiveness literature, primarily from a postsecondary education perspective. The researcher seeks through the second set of literature to provide an overview of the state of governance and its relationship to the provision of institutional leadership.

Thirdly, the focus of the researcher shifts to research questions one and two, with a specific emphasis on the understanding and practice of boards regarding shared leadership and board effectiveness.

Fourthly, with the focus on research questions three and five, the researcher seeks to explore the relationship between nonprofit governance and institutional performance. Additionally, this section provides a review of the literature associated with the linkage between nonprofit governance and the larger rural community.

Fifthly, looking at research question four, the researcher examines the change process involved in renewing and re-engineering board governance towards a shared leadership way of thinking and working together. This section provides a specific focus on the role of servant leadership in the context of the president's competency and performance. This is the first of the four factors seen to be associated with the practice of shared leadership and board effectiveness.

Lastly, the researcher explores the other three factors – the board's human capital composition, the board's governance-related education and training, and the board's view of themselves as stewards and as listeners to the college's voice. These three factors may be instrumental in affecting the improvement of board effectiveness.

Introduction

Background

Bugg and Dallhoff (2006), in *The National Study of Board Governance Practices in The Nonprofit and Voluntary Sector of Canada*, reported that these two sectors are comprised of 161,000 organizations with some $112 billion in revenues annually, representing approximately 10% of Canada's gross domestic product. The researchers discovered that, while organizations in the nonprofit sector may differ widely in size, mission and the ways in which they serve the community, they share common issues and challenges. In fact, the lines have blurred considerably between the public sector, the private sector, and the nonprofit sector. Osborne and Gaebler (1993) stated:

> There are very few services, traditionally provided by the public sector, that are not today provided somewhere by the private sector – and vice versa. Businesses are running public schools and fire departments, and nonprofit organizations, or the third sector, are rehabilitating convicts, running banks, and developing real estate (p. 43).

What is a Nonprofit Organization?

The Panel on Accountability and Governance in the Voluntary Sector (1999) defined a nonprofit organization as follows:

> An organization that serves a public benefit, depends on volunteers at least for its governance, has limited direct control by governments, other than in relation to tax benefits, and is not profit making, thus eligible for exemption from paying taxes. Although the term, nonprofit sector, is an encompassing concept

that includes registered charities as well as advocacy organizations, trade and professional associations and other nonprofits, we distinguish between nonprofit organizations and registered charities on the basis of their status under the federal Income Tax Act (p. 66).

Other significant distinctions exist in their ongoing challenge to attract and sustain resources and expertise. As noted in Wikipedia (2007) capacity building is an ongoing problem faced by nonprofit organizations that rely on external funding to maintain their operations. On occasion, these problems may serve to compromise the values and purpose of the organization. As reinforced in Ryan's essay, in *Nonprofit Governance and Management* (2002):

> The greatest peril is not that nonprofits may ultimately be driven out of the social services marketplace, rather, the danger is that in their struggle to become more viable competitors in the short term, nonprofit organizations will be forced to compromise the very assets that made them so vital to society in the first place (p. 14).

Change management becomes a way of life to many nonprofit organizations, their boards, and leaders. According to Keri Peoppe, In McNamara (2007), "devolution brings many challenges to nonprofit leaders. They must operate more effectively in the face of reduced funding. They must consider substantial changes in the way they have operated. Concepts such as strategic alliances and restructuring will become commonplace" (p. 5). So, too, has the consideration of governance reform found its way into mainstream nonprofit organizational theory. Friedman (2006) purported:

A decision to develop as the world becomes flat, is really a decision to focus on getting three basic things right: the infrastructure to connect more of your people with the flat-world platform; the right education to get more of your people innovating and collaborating on the flat-world platform; and the right governance – from fiscal policy to the rule of law – to manage the flow between your people and the flat-world platform in the most productive way possible (p. 398).

Interestingly, according to Wood (1996), in her introduction to *Nonprofit Boards and Leadership*, contemporary conceptions of governance in nonprofits have their antecedents in higher education in the 1960s. At that time, governance implied the so-called dual organization of faculty and administration. Within that structure, the faculty claimed authority to control the curriculum, the administration was expected to listen to faculty about any administrative policy or decision that impinged upon the education program.

Increased Demand for Good Governance

In today's environment of globalization, urbanization, heightened competition, and increased demands for good governance standards and guidelines, nonprofit boards are under pressure to become more effective in their governance role. As indicated by the Province of Alberta in their recently published Board Governance Discussion Paper (2007), "Accountability, transparency, and independence are part of a trend to strengthen corporate, nonprofit and public service governance across Canada" (p. 3). A Task Force has been mandated to develop an inventory of existing agencies, boards, and commissions [ABCs], which include the boards of postsecondary institutions, consult with stakeholders, and submit a report with recommendations for the

Premier's consideration in the early fall of 2007. In the same paper, it was reported that the Government of Alberta has created more than 130 ABCs to which it allocates more than 55% of government expenses. The decisions and activities of the ABC's affect a wide range of public policy objectives in crucial areas such as promoting advanced research, regulating the energy industry, and providing postsecondary education and health care.

According to Carter and Man (2003), accountability requires good governance from the nonprofit sector as much, or more, than in the private sector. In the profit sector, corporations are primarily accountable to their stakeholders for the ability of the corporation to return a profit. In the nonprofit sector, however, organizations are accountable to their members as well as to the general public. For example, as outlined by Calder and Andrews (1984), the Saskatchewan Roughriders of the Canadian Football League are a community owned nonprofit organization. They are governed by a six person volunteer board and 52 committees, comprised of literally thousands of active members. These volunteers are responsible for such diverse initiatives as season ticket sales, marketing, alumni activities, event sponsors, and many social events.

Wood (1996), in her introduction to *Nonprofit Boards and Leadership*, purported that stakeholders external to a nonprofit may include public and private funders, elected and appointed government officials and their staffs, families or other advocates of the recipients of services, accrediting organizations, professional organizations; any neighborhood, city or other community of which an organization is perceived to be a part, and increasingly,

21

the media. These external stakeholders are the same people that constitute the majority of the membership of the Roughriders.

The United Way of Canada's Board Basics Manual (2007), outlined four possible board governance models, which include the policy board, the policy governance board, the working/administrative board, and the collective board. For instance, relative to the collective model, vision, planning and evaluation are shared value based, with shared responsibility for policy setting. Similarly, from a fiscal perspective, the board and staff work on financial matters as a team. As supported by the United Way of Canada, decisions in the collective model are consensus-based, with all members representing the enterprise to the various communities.

However, recent governance-related issues have arisen in recent years, due to the collapse of organizations such as Enron and WorldCom. As outlined by Gill (2002), issues which will not be tolerated included a lack of board accountability, inaccessible board members, confusion amongst members, limited access to information, and a general mindset that would disallow public participation in board functions. Hence, in response to a need for more engaged and strategic governance, according to the Johns Hopkins Nonprofit Listening Post Project (2005), a growing movement has emerged advocating a more managerial model, in which the board itself is active in managerial functions. These functions may include setting the salary for all managerial staff, reviewing internal organizational practices, and setting and monitoring performance at the program level. According to the Internet Nonprofit Centre, accessed online, the distinction between governance and management is not absolute. Thus, these domains are not considered mutually exclusive, as there appears to be much overlap between the two.

Governance and Stakeholders

The willingness to develop relationships and confer with internal and external stakeholders has long been a fundamental role of governance. In this regard, Carver (1997) introduced the idea of moral ownership. He observed that in a nonprofit setting, good governance is accountable to all stakeholders. As well, as suggested by Wood (1996), in her introduction to *Nonprofit Boards and Leadership*, internal stakeholders matter, as well. They may include service recipients such as students, employees, and the governing board itself.

The affairs of every nonprofit organization must be directed, managed, and supported. These duties are an important part of what is called governance. The Panel on Accountability and Governance in the Voluntary Sector (1999) posited that the overall goal of governance is the protection of the public interest. O'Callaghan and Korbin (2000) contended that this responsibility is achieved by the creation of a set of rules, which in turn creates a structure and allocates power to responsible parties. The structure is created by the legal and administrative framework within which a nonprofit organization functions. This may include the organization's governing statutes, the articles and by-laws, resolutions of the board and other policies and procedures which are adopted by the organization. Doing governance, as noted by the same Panel (1999) is the domain of the board of directors, which, in the nonprofit sector, is normally comprised of volunteers. For example, as recorded in the 1995 Canada Games

Final Report (1995), as president of the host society, our organization chart reflected 16 major functionalities, which were overseen by volunteer vice-presidents. In actuality, these 16 leaders spawned a paid staff complement of 120 people, and a volunteer organization of close to 8000 volunteers.

In recent times, the increased attention on, and the need for, the aforementioned constitutional elements have served to raise the bar for nonprofit organizations. Many nonprofit organizations are making an attempt to improve their governance. Some are achieving success in increasing board effectiveness. However, to make matters even more challenging for nonprofit organizations, The National Study of Board Governance (2006) identified two emerging trends in board governance: (1) increased focus on governance, and (2) increased demand for, and reduced supply of, qualified directors.

Knowledge about Governance

With an increased focus on governance comes a need to improve the board's knowledge about governance. As outlined by Bugg and Dallhoff (2006), 73% of respondents reported that they had a continuous training and development program in place. When asked to rate the program, 31% rated it as poor, 42% as satisfactory, 22% as good and only 6% rated it as excellent. Less engaged boards indicated fewer programs available and rated existing programs lower. Any team that is engaged and wants to win the championship, as suggested by Andringa and Engstrom (2002), in their *Nonprofit Board Answer Book,* takes care to select, orient, and train its members. Similarly, The Society of Corporate Secretaries and Governance Professionals, in their article,

Governance for Nonprofits: From Little League to Universities, accessed online, in citing the personal qualities of board members critical to a successful operation, commented on knowledge. The Society noted that knowledge of your constituents, operations, organization, and managerial acumen is a basic quality of a good board member.

In fact, The United Way of Canada (2007), as accessed on their board development website, indicated that the courts have said that it is no longer possible to be a passive director. Lack of knowledge or passive participation will not absolve a board member of legal responsibility. For instance, all vice presidents associated with the 1995 Canada Games host society were obliged to interface with their respective counterparts at both the 1991 Canada Winter Games, in Charlottetown, Prince Edward Island, and the 1993 Canada Summer Games, hosted in Kamloops, British Columbia. Additionally, all directors were required to submit to human resources, an outline of the responsibilities for their associate vice-president, prior to recruiting for the position.

Recruitment and Diversity

With an increased demand for, and a reduced supply of, qualified directors comes a need to improve a board's human capital recruitment practices. The National Study of Board Governance (2006) reported that 58% of respondents reported that their recruitment process was effective and that they had a number of qualified prospects to choose from each year. This is in contrast to 31% who reported having difficulty filling board seats. In relation to the diversity and expertise required, the same study (2006) noted when respondents were asked to identify, from a list the areas of expertise needed to be added to their board, they most commonly selected marketing and communications (52%), followed by fundraising (48%), strategic planning (44%), government relations (33%), risk management (31%), donor stewardship (29%), community relations (28%), technology (25%), finance (25%), accounting (20%), and investment (15%). Fifty-three percent reported that their boards have the skill set necessary to evaluate a potential merger, 29% reported that they do not have the skill set, and 18% were unsure. Fifty-seven percent reported that 50% or more of their board members have the ability to read and understand financial statements. In a related study, Salamon and Geller (2005) indicated increased board member expertise was required in fundraising and advocacy. Although 70 of the nonprofit organizations reported that their boards were highly or significantly involved in fundraising, a third of the chief executive officers indicated they would welcome increased board involvement in this function. In contrast, only 43% of the nonprofit organizations indicated that their boards were highly or significantly involved in advocacy efforts, well below other strategic functions. While the current level of board involvement in advocacy was accepted by most nonprofit executives, over a quarter (28%) of them indicated they would like to see more board involvement in this function.

In discussing planning for the succession and diversity of the board, Carter and Man (2003) recommended, in appointing new directors, it is important to ensure the diversity of the board, making sure that the directors bring a variety of useful and relevant expertise to the operations of the corporation. In linking human capital composition and recruitment to board effectiveness, O'Callaghan and Korbin (2000) suggested a clearly defined process for annually reviewing the composition of the board and establishing board membership criteria which are linked to the current trends of the organization.

One such important criterion is accountability. Strengthening accountability provisions has been a definite focus of nonprofit organizations in recent years, as studied by Salamon and Geller (2005). Almost half of the nonprofit organizations reported that they had adopted or strengthened their procedures to prevent fraud and/or enhance organizational accountability over the previous two years. Interestingly, a limited number of organizations, who made changes in their accountability practices, did so because of funder demands, media attention, or other outside pressures. More commonly, the reasons for change were related to a desire to ensure transparency and accountability (52%), to demonstrate effectiveness (46%), and to serve customers and clients better (36%).

Many boards remain government organizations that must be accountable, effective, and subject to legitimate government direction. Indeed, many of these nonprofit organizations have taken over many functions in respect to public welfare, which were formerly considered to be the government's responsibility. As noted by Waide, in his essay in, *Nonprofit Governance and Management* (2002), many nonprofit organizations must cooperate and compete with for-profit organizations in new ways. Hence the changing marketplace demands new ways of leading, complete with a new set of governance skills, knowledge and abilities.

A Competent CEO

Yale's Peter Dobkin Hall (2006) suggested that the nonprofit sector changes constantly in scale and scope. In order to manage these changes and ensure effectiveness, board members need to position a competent management team, normally led by a chief executive officer [CEO]. Often, the CEO can be instrumental in helping the board towards a deeper understanding of advances in organizational governance. Eadie (2006) in the article, *Making a Good Board Better*, maintained that the superintendent was anything but a bystander. As a High-Impact Governing Task Force member, he was involved in all deliberations, and he ensured his board members were an integral part of the process. It was recognized that detailed involvement in the process was a concrete sign of his commitment to top notch district governance. It would appear that leadership in a nonprofit organization takes the form of involvement and commitment, rather than direction. The former CEO of the J. Paul Getty Trust, Harold Williams, in Silverman and Taliento (2006), said, "You will have little opportunity to lead by making decisions. You'll have the power of the budget to some extent, but if you have a vision or you want to make any changes, you're going to do it by leadership and by inspiration and not by direction – you've got to be a Pied Piper" (p. 40). Similarly, former White House deputy chief of staff and university president, Philip Lader, in Silverman and Taliento (2006), offered:

Have a passion for that organization's mission. Otherwise, the frustrations just wouldn't be worth it. Recognize that everything is consensus building. Know that you have the affirmative responsibility to project in every setting the critical importance of what the organization does – to funders, to media, to potential volunteers, to all constituents (p. 40).

Robert W. Galvin, former team member of the chief executive office, Motorola Corporation, in Collins and Porras (2002) confessed, "One responsibility (we) considered paramount is seeing to the continuity of capable senior leadership. We have always striven to have proven backup candidates available, employed transition training programs to best prepare prime candidates, and been very open (succession planning). Thus, we believe that continuity is immensely valuable" (p. 169). Clearly, a daunting set of instructive pointers coming from the private sector for a nonprofit organization without effective governance practices.

Bugg and Dallhoff (2006) observed that 80% of respondents reported that they were satisfied that the CEO is properly overseen, guided and supported to achieve his or her goals as set by the board. Asked about performance evaluation, 71% reported that they conduct a formal evaluation of the CEO based on pre-set criteria. Once again, less engaged boards found this more of a challenge. As well, with reference to the size of the challenges, Andringa and Engstrom (2002) stated, "In today's world, the board and CEO of a nonprofit organization, typically, have a greater leadership challenge than their for-profit or government counterparts" (p. xii).

From a governance perspective, a significant portion of the leadership challenge is transformational thinking and working together. As intimated by Peters and Waterman (1982), a team needs to focus on a transforming purpose. To do so, according to Burns (1978), the team will need a transforming leader; one who exhibits leadership that builds on man's need for meaning, and one who exhibits leadership that creates institutional purpose. James Brian Quinn (1977) said:

> Championships will go to the (nonprofit) organization that has slowly discovered that their most effective goal is to be best at certain things. We now try to get our people to help us work out, what these things should be, how to define best objectively, and how to become best in our selected spheres. You would be surprised at how motivating that can be. (p. 26)

Accountability, Transparency, and Stewardship

Unlike private corporations, as outlined in the Government of Alberta's Board Governance Review Discussion Paper (2007), the public sector entities are created by government to address a public policy mandate. Therefore, their purposes are public. They are to act in the best interests of the people. In a sense, all residents are stakeholders and in many cases the government is the sole shareholder. Thus, in the public sector, the achievement of effective governance should necessitate being accountable, and transparent in their actions, to all people. This necessitates listening on a regular basis to a diverse group of citizens. Likewise, effective governance should require balancing two domains. They are as follows: (1) the government's desired level of accountability, and (2) the nonprofit's work conducted at an arms length from government.

The balancing act is clearly the essence of the art and science of governance in the nonprofit sector. In 1997, the United Nations, as submitted by Carter and Man (2003), published a list of characteristics of good governance, which included:

1. Participation in decision making and reaching broad consensus on what is in the best interest of the organization;
2. Responsive, effective and efficient performance;
3. Equity and sound rule of law;
4. Strategic planning; and
5. Accountability and transparency.

Bugg and Dallhoff (2006) noted several major trends in board governance. One such trend was an increased demand for transparency and accountability. Three reasons were cited for this trend. They include: (1) more emphasis on process, (2) increased formality in financial audits, and (3) more boards make in-camera sessions standard practice. In response to these reasons, the aforementioned Study outlined five implications and challenges for nonprofit boards. They are as follows: (1) bearing increased cost of meeting higher standards, (2) balancing implementation of standards with resources, (3) ensuring compliance, (4) determining the board's information needs and formulating the right questions to ask, and (5) formalizing accountability and stewardship.

The formalization of accountability and stewardship begins with cohesiveness and mutual trust. O'Callaghan and Korbin (2000) submitted that the board of a nonprofit organization must assume responsibility for the stewardship of the entity and, as part of the overall stewardship responsibility, assume responsibility for the following matters:

1. Selecting, evaluating, rewarding and, if necessary, removing the CEO, and ensuring that the appropriate senior management success plans are in place;
2. Approving the organization's strategic direction and evaluating its progress;
3. Ensuring legal and ethical conduct by the organization's officers and employees;
4. Identifying the principal risks of the organization's business and ensuring the implementation of appropriate systems to manage these risks;
5. Ensuring a communications policy is in place for the organization; and
6. Ensuring the integrity of the organization's internal control and management information systems.

The nonprofit sector's challenges with funding shortages and a lack of training make building effective organizations difficult. Thus, from a customer service perspective, stewardship can be seen through an economic frame. Judy Vredenburgh, former CEO of Big Brothers, Big Sisters, and former Senior Vice President of March of Dimes, in Silverman and Taliento (2006) offered, "every time we in nonprofits satisfy customers, we drain resources, and every time for-profits satisfy a customer, they get resources back. That sounds very simple, but it has huge implications, and I don't think the for-profit people really get that" (p. 41). Simply stated, nonprofit organizations are difficult to run. As an explanation, Williams, in Silverman and Taliento (2006) offered:

> Because they are more hand-to-mouth, and because the quality and amount of staff is thinner than it is in a typical corporate environment. In many respects the typical nonprofit leader is much more entrepreneurial than the typical chief executive in the corporate world. You have fewer resources, fewer staff, and less certainty (p. 41).

Living from hand-to-mouth, as suggested by Gill (2001), requires five key considerations by boards if effective governance is the goal. They include: (1) vision, (2) direction, (3) resources, (4) monitoring, and (5) accountability. Vision is envisioning the future and developing a corporate mission that will be flexible and responsive to possible future challenges and opportunities. Direction denotes the setting of goals for the organization. Resources imply securing resources to achieve the desired results and realize the organization's vision and goals. Monitoring is periodically reviewing the relationship between the organization's resources and its vision and direction, ensuring that the organizational vehicle is well-maintained and progressing, within legal limits, towards its destination. Accountability is ensuring efficient use of resources and reporting progress and detours to the organization's stakeholders.

Measuring Board Effectiveness

Ways for measuring board effectiveness remain a big challenge for most boards. For example, the differentiation between organizational effectiveness and board effectiveness is problematic for most nonprofit boards. As well, the differentiation between qualitative and quantitative metrics is challenging for most nonprofit organizations wishing to engage in measuring their effectiveness. For example, in *Governance Matters* (2007), accessed online, benchmarks for effective boards are noted using a spirit and character frame of reference. They are as follows:

1. Passion for the mission;
2. First or second nonprofit organization;
3. Mutual trust;
4. Commitment to process;
5. Standards and aspirations;
6. Openness; and
7. Ethical sensitivity.

However, the National Study of Board Governance Practices in the Nonprofit and Voluntary Sector in Canada (2006) reported a quantitative-like sampling of responses on measuring board effectiveness which included:

1. Evaluate the board based on agreed-upon board practices, as described in the board's policies and procedures manual;
2. Measure the effectiveness of board meetings;
3. Determine stakeholder satisfaction through a survey;

4. Determine if fundraising levels are meeting set targets;

5. Determine if board members have signed off on all appropriate board policies;

6. Set board goals, measure success in reaching them and building milestones into the process;

7. Distinguish between measuring the board and measuring the organization;

8. Measure over time;

9. Determine the percentage of the strategic plan that has been completed;

10. Use qualitative as well as quantitative measures;

11. Set expectations for board members and evaluate performance on that basis;

12. Design an annual work plan, monitor it and evaluate it based on accomplishments; and

13. Hold annual peer, board, and individual board member assessments.

In comparison, what might an ineffective board look like? The Canadian Union of Public Employees [CUPE] National Research Branch (2007), as accessed online, stated, "it is easy to spot a board in trouble" (p. 7). The more prominent warning signs are as follows:

1. Excessive turnover of executive directors/CEOs or board members;

2. Difficulty in recruiting credible board members;

3. Chronic deficits;

4. Low attendance or participation in board meetings;

5. Failure to address conflicts of interest; and

6. Poor communications with funding agencies and stakeholders.

The aforementioned Research Branch (2007) continued:

> Poorly run boards give rise to unaccountable practices, non-transparency, and poor communications with workers, clients, the public, and funding agencies. Ineffective governance imposes a level of dysfunction upon an agency and can eventually lead to organizational failure (p. 7).

Major Themes

The Province of Alberta, in their Board Governance Review Discussion Paper (2007) posited several 'good governance' themes, which formed the basis for public consultation. They included role and responsibilities, selection and succession, the independence of board members, board committee structure, director liability, transparency, and types of boards. Relative to the role and responsibility theme, the paper suggested that a strong and effective board should have a clear view of its role in relation to management. Secondly, in terms of selection and succession, the paper noted while boards do different things in every organization, all boards can better carry out their core responsibilities by ensuring that they have the right people to meet their mandate. Thirdly, with reference to the independence of board members, the paper implied that in keeping with emerging leading practices, boards must move beyond traditional advisory roles to become active players that take initiative in the exercise of their oversight responsibilities. Fourthly, regarding board committee structure, the paper stated that leading practices suggest that boards should establish committees that enhance effectiveness by ensuring

36

focus on matters of particular concern. Fifthly, with respect to director liability, the paper posited that liability and risk are more important than ever, given the numerous court cases involving mismanagement of investor's funds, and the efforts of the private sector to develop legislation that will curb such mismanagement (e.g. in 2003, Ontario adopted Bill 198, which focuses on the reliability of corporate disclosures and the ease with which investors can launch class action law suits). Sixthly, focusing on transparency, the paper offered that transparency helps an organization demonstrate what it is doing, and that it is being done in an appropriate and ethical manner. Lastly, with reference to types of boards, the paper stated that, in reviewing the different elements that contribute to good governance, it is clear that each board will need to tailor its governance practices to its specific location. Further, some types of boards may, as a group, need to take a different approach to certain governance issues.

Similarly, while organizations differed widely in size, mission, and the ways in which they serve the community, the findings of the National Study of Board Governance Practices in the Nonprofit and Voluntary Sector in Canada (2006) discovered they shared a common vision of the trends, issues, and challenges. The Study produced a number of themes which are noted below:

Leadership: the importance of the chair's leadership role and the importance of selecting and retaining the right CEO.

Recruitment: the challenge of recruiting and retaining qualified board members and the difficulty of dealing with board member appointments.

Succession Planning: the need to develop board leaders and plan for the succession of the CEO.

Role Clarity: the need for role clarity and ensuring that board members understand their fiduciary duties and responsibilities.

Education and Development: the importance of the continuous education and development of board members.

Accountability and Stewardship: the way in which higher expectations and increasing demands from donors and funders affect the board's role.

Culture: the importance of developing the right board culture and balancing the need for a successful board culture with the rigor of policies and processes.

Board Meetings: the importance of effective board meetings to carry out the work of the board and engage board members.

Strategic Planning: the need to understand fully the board's role in strategic planning and to increase board member competency in this area.

Performance Measurement: the lack of performance measures to assess board effectiveness.

Risk Management: the need for better risk management policies, processes, and tools.

Board Governance Effectiveness – An Overview

Initially, it is important to understand that board governance effectiveness, particularly in the nonprofit sector, is exceptionally rare and grossly misunderstood. Harvard University researchers, Chait, Holland, and Taylor (1996) stated that after 10 years of research and dozens of engagements as consultants to nonprofit boards, they have reached a rather stark conclusion: "effective governance by a board of trustees is a relatively rare and unnatural act" (p. 1). Likewise, noted management guru, Peter Drucker (1974) weighed in succinctly on the efficiency issue when he offered, "there is one thing all boards have in common, regardless of their legal position, "they do not function" (p. 628). Additionally, Carver (1997), whose groundbreaking policy governance model has influenced the way public and nonprofit boards operate around the world, commented on the misunderstanding issue from a governance perspective, when he offered, "here we confront a flagrant irony in management literature: where opportunity for leadership is greatest, yet job design for leadership is poorest" (p. 8).

Even though it is arguable that today's boards receive more data, demand more justification for managerial decision-making, and quite frankly, take their roles more seriously; there is a general recognition that improvements in board governance effectiveness have not kept pace with the changing times. In fact, Walter Salmon (2000), who counts over 30 years of corporate board experience, when writing in the Harvard Business Review on Corporate Governance, offered this comment relative to the need for keeping pace, "there are still many unexploited opportunities for boards to improve [corporate] performance rather than simply confining themselves to mopping up after disasters" (p. 3).

Therefore, why does there appear to be more energy spent in the boardroom(s) 'mopping up' rather than on 'purposing, engaging and enriching' the governance process? Likewise, why does there appear to be a gap in understanding regarding how boards define themselves and actually think and work collectively?

Simply stated, with reference to the 'mopping up' conundrum, the so-called "tides of trusteeship", a term coined by Chait, Holland and Taylor (1996), seem to take boards in the wrong directions. For example, the tides take them from strategy towards operations, from long-term challenges towards immediate concerns, from collective action toward individual initiatives (p. 1). Thus, unless interventions are considered and/or built, implemented and sustained, it is reasonable to assume that boards will have great difficulty in achieving effective board governance.

Additionally, in response to the 'gap in understanding and knowledge question', Lang (2005) suggested that boards are often defined by their relationship and connectivity to the CEO and management. As well, Carter and Carter (1997), in offering an explanation to the lack of certainty question, posited how a board can simultaneously govern and work at operations borders on contradiction. Hence, unless one accepts the possibility of the board's connection to senior administration, as some form of high governance tool, governing and working at operations become extremely contradictory, and tends to disperse rather than consolidate participation and thus, board governance effectiveness.

Understanding and Practice – Research Questions 1 & 2

The road to becoming a policy governing board in the public nonprofit college sector is normally paved with understanding and practice. Many talented individuals come to their role as a higher education board member with corporate and/or operating board experience, however little to no experience in policy governance in the nonprofit sector. Chait, Holland, and Taylor (1996) outlined the four major obstacles faced by these talented individuals, when they encounter their first exposure to nonprofit policy governance. They are as follows:

1. Dispassionate Analysts and Impassioned Advocates – i.e. board members are expected to rise above parochial interests and personal biases in order to make decisions that are in the best interests of the long-term welfare of the institution. However, at the same time, the administration desires board members to be committed, psychologically and financially, to the institution.

2. Part-Time Amateurs and Full-Time Professionals – i.e. from a board member's perspective, the institution may resemble a foreign culture with different mores, strange customs, and odd values. As part-time amateurs, board members do not feel especially well-equipped to oversee the work of full-time professionals and to be ultimate arbiters of a prudent course of action.

3. All-Stars and No Constellation – i.e. board members are, almost by definition, conspicuously successful and often powerful and influential individuals, accustomed to leadership roles. To compound the problem, most boards rarely practice as a team, as board members customarily meet to govern, not to rehearse.

4. Low Stakes and High Rollers – i.e. with rare exceptions, there are few penalties for the sins of misgovernance, especially compared with the punishments attached to the sins of mismanagement. Even if the institution falters, board members can avert personal embarrassment and humiliation. Few board members lose much sleep over trusteeship, even though the caliber of governance that the trustees provide has profound consequences for the institution.

Dr. Cindra Smith, the Director of Trustee Education Services of the Community College League of California, and a committed disciple of noted governance guru, John Carver, is requested to facilitate numerous higher education board retreats, workshops, and seminars every year. Generally, the requests come from postsecondary policy boards, which may be characterized as the aforementioned "all stars, dispassionate analysts, and part-time amateurs" (p. 11). Normally, they seek a fuller understanding of the concepts of leadership and governance, within a college environment. During such a retreat in Alberta, in October 2001, in her summarization of the theory surrounding effective board governance, she offered the following suggestions to the board in an attempt to improve their understanding of their role and responsibilities:

1. Focus on policy and institutional performance;
2. Provide proactive, visionary leadership;
3. Be externally focused;
4. Shape institutional direction;
5. Assure that the mission is achieved;
6. Understand that issues are complex;
7. Be cohesive while seeing multiple perspectives; and
8. Ensure you are learning constantly.

It may not be coincidental that Dr. Smith's eight suggestions begin with a call for boards and administrators to focus on policy development and institutional performance. Within the context of policy making and monitoring is the daunting governance responsibility of facilitating the shaping of the institution's ends statements, otherwise known as the values, vision, mission and outcomes. In fact, Houle (1989), prescribed the ultimate test of board effectiveness is how effectively the board ensures that the mission of their institution is achieved.

Just as many talented individuals arrive at their first policy governance role, with little to no experience in policy governance, the same may be said for their lack of background in shared leadership. In many cases, new board members come to their first nonprofit governance experience with only a classical leadership understanding and cursory practice with operational/administrative boards.

Nemerowicz and Rosi (1997) outlined the six major differences between the two predominant leadership approaches within a governance context. They are as follows:

1. Shared leadership is identified by the quality of the member's interactions rather than their position. Classical leadership is displayed by a member's position in a group or hierarchy.

2. Shared leadership is evaluated by how members work together. Classical leadership is evaluated by whether the leader solves problems.

3. Shared leadership seeks to enhance the process and to make it more fulfilling. Classical leadership provides the solutions and the answers.

4. Shared leadership calls for members to become independent. All are active participants, [including both board members and administration], in the process of leadership. Classical leadership recognizes distinct differences between leaders and followers.

5. Shared leadership communication is crucial with a stress on conversation. Classical leadership communication is often formal.

6. Shared leadership values democratic processes, honesty, and shared ethics. It seeks a common good. Classical leadership often relies on secrecy, deception, and payoffs (p. 16).

Consequently, if one were to assume that the board members and administration collectively chose to subscribe to the theory and practice of shared leadership, wherein would lie another developmental challenge in governance? Harvard's Richard Chait (2005) argued that their challenge would lie somewhere along the fault-line determination between the role of the board and the administration. Chait offered the following differentiations, as a keynote presenter, in Regina, Saskatchewan, at the 2005 Governance Now Conference:

1. In the traditional governance model, diagnosis is a problem of performance. The board's response is to codify their role, clarify their tasks and their objective is to do the work better.
2. In the reframed governance model, diagnosis is a problem of purpose. The board's response is to enrich the job, engage the board and their objective is to do better work.

Embracing a reframed understanding of the theoretical foundation and the associated concepts of board governance effectiveness and shared leadership will normally necessitate a major change in how the board members and administration think about governance. As well, it would require an adjustment as to how they think when they govern. Carver (1997) suggested that policy governance offers not a mere improvement in board leadership, but a revolution in board room behavior, and in the governance-management relationship. Furthermore, it cannot be implemented by changing language or by making a few adjustments. Carver (1997) posited that, should the board wish to embrace the theoretical foundation and use this more sophisticated model of governance, they must not only understand the theory, but also be prepared for major changes in actual behavior, appearances, and practice (p. 33).

The basic rationale for the consideration of governance as shared leadership is apparent, when considering the key global trends bombarding the higher education system today. Dr. Ron Faris (2006), who is credited with the development of the Saskatchewan Regional College System, in speaking to the Rural North American Conference, in Calgary, on the development of learning communities, offered three key inter-related drivers of change: (1) globalization, (2) technological change, and (3) new knowledge and learning. In addition, Dr. Faris acknowledged the transformation from a resource-based to a knowledge-based economy, and, in doing so, noted the emerging need for the consideration of human and social capital and new literacies. His operative definition of learning communities is worthy of inclusion, as it has significant rural higher education and aboriginal connotations, in the sense of communities of place. Neighborhoods, villages, towns, cities, or regions that explicitly use lifelong learning as an organizing principle and social/cultural goal in order to promote collaboration of their civic, economic, public, voluntary, and education sectors to enhance social, economic, and environmental conditions on a sustainable, inclusive basis.

Faris (2006) posited that the linkage between higher education leadership and the larger community's growth as a community of place has several purposes. Primarily, such a place, which is supported by college leadership, seeks to build community capacity in the forms of human and social capital and infrastructure. As well, a "community of place" seeks to bridge that support to the social inclusion of minorities and under-served populations. Additionally,

46

it was suggested that learning communities of place seek to drive the sustainable triple bottom line – environmental, economic, and social/cultural development.

It is purported that effective board governance has a key role to play in the development of these learning communities of place. Also, it would appear that a classical leadership approach may not be sufficient given the driving forces of the information age. Senge (1990) suggested that the basic rationale for such organizations is that in situations of rapid change only those that are flexible, adaptive, and productive will excel. For this to happen, he argued that organizations need to "discover how to tap people's commitment and capacity to learn at all levels" (p. 89).

Effectively tapping people's commitment and capacity, at all levels of a rural college community, would necessitate a board and administration thinking and working collectively, in more than one mode. Chait (2005) suggested three sequential modes of thinking and working together as a board. They are the fiduciary mode, the strategic mode, and the generative mode. He purported that the value added by a board increases as the board becomes more proficient in more than one mode and develops the ability to work in the generative mode.

The biggest part of the governance problem such that a board may engage the larger community, may be structural in nature. Senge (1990) suggested that while all people have the capacity to learn, the structures in which they have to function are often not conducive to reflection and engagement. Similarly, a policy governance board may not be equipped to handle the rigors of the information age and the development of a learning community of place. Senge

(1990) purported that people may lack the tools and guiding ideas to make sense of the situations they face. Organizations that are continually expanding their capacity to create their future require a fundamental shift of mind among their members.

Another perspective relative to properly equipping the board and administration for their shared leadership role in the development of a learning community is offered by Drucker (1974), who indicated that because the players in an information-based organization are specialists, they cannot be told how to do their work. As well, he offered the analogy of the conductor and the horn player for our consideration, when he suggested that there are probably few conductors who could even coax one note out of a French horn, let alone show the horn player how to do it. But, the conductor can focus the horn player's skill and knowledge on the musician's joint performance.

To make a difference in higher education awareness, participation, and attainment, within the community at large, the board and administration may need to see themselves as stewards. Block (1993) called for a new way of thinking about the workplace – arguing that notions of leadership and management need replacing by that of stewardship. Also, it is argued that [nonprofit] organizations should replace traditional management tools of control and consistency with partnership and choice. Lastly, individuals, who see themselves as stewards, will choose responsibility over entitlement and hold themselves accountable to those over whom they exercise power. In short there appears to be a need, within board governance, for the demonstration of leadership by choosing service, or stewardship, over self-interest.

Relationship of Institutional Performance to Governance

One of the primary roles of a policy board is the monitoring of institutional performance. Indeed, it is accepted, within policy governance, that when a board monitors the performance of the institution, they are monitoring the performance of their only employee, the president. Additionally, it is accepted within the context of policy governance, that when a board monitors the performance of the institution, they are, in fact, monitoring their own performance, as the originators and facilitators of the development of the institution's ends statements. Dr. Smith (2001) stated that it is the board's job to assure performance. This does not imply that they are responsible to do the work, but it is implicit that they assure it is done. Furthermore, they assure performance, via monitoring and the use of policy goals and standards to evaluate performance. In fact, it is generally accepted that it is these policy goals, which are used by the president, to develop the framework underpinning the college's business plan, within the board established set of executive limitations.

Dr. Smith (2001) purported that it is the board's leadership responsibility to provide clear delegation to their president, thus avoiding the 'react and ratify' syndrome. This responsibility requires thoughtful and thorough exploration of the board's values, along with a clear differentiation of ends and means. She suggested that the result of such behaviors should be the empowerment of all groups along with the public dissemination of the board's ends statements, or the values, vision, mission, and outcomes.

49

As an example of a community focused ends statement, it was offered, by Dr. Smith (2001), "that it is because of your college, in a rural setting, that the community will have an employable adult population with the work-force skills necessary for employment at the family-wage level" (p. 12). In achieving this end, it would follow that the president would endeavor to focus on the means. Hence, it is about the building of the necessary strategies, action plans, and resources to deliver on the intent of the ends statement in a timely fashion. Likewise, it would follow that the board, in concert with administration, would endeavor to monitor the performance of the president [and institution] in the achievement of the ends.

As was alluded to earlier, the fundamental societal transformation from the industrial age to the information age, and the corresponding challenges and opportunities it presents for higher education, are driving a need for higher accountability of institutional performance and board governance reform. A report representing the results of a two-year study by the Commission on National Investment in Higher Education (1998) recommended institutions of higher learning should make major structural changes in their accountability and transparency systems so that decision makers can assess the relative value of departments, programs, and systems in order to reallocate scarce resources. Additionally, the report recommended as a part of the overall re-structuring, colleges and universities should pursue greater mission differentiation to streamline their services and better respond to the changing needs of their constituencies.

Performance measures, derived from the ends statements, have become the primary institutional performance methodology to track the transformation of higher education, and some may argue, board governance reform. As outlined in *A Learning Alberta* (2006), Alberta Advanced Education annually assesses five key performance indicators, which are tracked and aggregated into a scorecard and then used to award incremental revenues to higher performing institutions. These key performance indicators reflect three specific ministerial outcomes. They are as follows: (1) responsiveness, (2) accessibility, and (3) affordability. Correspondingly, the indicators for responsiveness include employment rate and graduate satisfaction. Accessibility is a stand-alone indicator and simply measures incremental enrolment growth using a three-year rolling average. Lastly, affordability is represented by two indicators which are administrative expenses and enterprise revenue.

The case for board governance reform and accountability becomes more acute when one considers that institution and community performance are now being measured on a regular basis by stakeholders, other than college officials. In short, Canadians have become more aware of the wide range of significant benefits derived from lifelong learning, such as economic, health, environmental, and income. Nationally, Canada has recently completed a composite learning index, through the Canadian Council on Learning (2006), which seeks to combine a variety of statistical indicators to produce an overall score and measure lifelong learning that goes beyond just formal education. The data needs to be pan-Canadian, available at the regional/provincial level, reliable, and collected on a regular basis. Examples of the performance indicators include the following:

1. Student skills in reading, mathematics and problem solving;
2. Dropout rates;
3. University attainment;
4. Postsecondary attendance;
5. Adult participation in job-related training;
6. Availability of training in the workplace;
7. Access to learning organizations;
8. Volunteering;
9. Charitable donations;
10. Spending on memberships and organizations;
11. Access to community organizations;
12. Spending on reading materials;
13. Spending on the internet;
14. Spending on sports;
15. Spending on arts; and
16. Spending on museums.

Clearly, given the plethora of emerging internal and external accountabilities, board governance cannot continue to drift with the tides. It would appear that the days may be numbered for boards that choose to dispatch an agenda of micro-management issues tied in some fashion to the here and now issues as opposed to the institution's strategic priorities. In this regard, Chait, Holland, and Taylor (1996) argued that unless counter forces are initiated and sustained, the board will not achieve effective governance. This state is defined as a collective effort, utilizing smooth and reliable processes, which shape the actions that advance a shared purpose consistent with the institution's mission.

As well, given the apparent need to purpose, engage, and transform the governance process towards some form of shared leadership, the reader is reminded of the challenges associated with redefining the role of the board and, who exactly will facilitate the transformation and lead these processes.

Hemann (1999) suggested that the role of the board is frequently an inherited one, and without a conscious effort to analyze its role, assess its philosophy, and determine what outcomes are needed from the board members' work, the future board is destined to be a reflection of its predecessors. Therefore, three questions arise: Who is responsible for the identification of a need to change? Who is responsible for the planning and design of the case for change? Who is responsible for driving and sustaining the process of governance renewal?

To reverse the cycle, as cited by Hemann (1999), a policy board, such as those which govern the rural, public Colleges of Western Canada, must first plan for the change. It is purported by Hemann that the planning process begins with the president, in concert with his or her board chairperson. Hence, Hemann signaled our review of the first proposition, consistent with research question four, which explores the extent of the contribution of each of the four variables towards board governance effectiveness.

The Four Factors – Research Question 4

Factor One – The President's Competency and Performance

Carver (1997) advised boards to commence the renewal process by obsessing on the ends and warns of the deleterious influence of conventional wisdom. For example, it has been noted that a traditional or operational orientation to governance can be narrow (Skinner, 1986; Crosby, 1989; Deming, 1986). All aforementioned investigators are in agreement that an [board's] obsession with fiduciary responsibilities may produce a narrowness of vision. In contrast, Carver (1997) took governance to a higher plain and posited leadership within the governance process as a moral challenge, which requires member commitment, understanding, and knowledge.

Historically, governance cultures have not welcomed nor accommodated social change to any significant degree. As Ferguson (1980) stated, "it is not changing itself as much as that place in between that we fear ... [as] there is nothing to hold on to" (p. 209). That 'place in between' requires leaders, as articulated by Collins and Porras (1994), in their well-developed treatise, *Built to Last*, to think less in terms of being a brilliant visionary, or seeking the personality characteristics of charismatic leadership, and to think more in terms of being an organizational visionary and building the characteristics of a visionary organization (p. 41). In relation to the role of the president in the renewal process, it is noted that neither Thomas Jefferson, nor John Adams, was a charismatic visionary leader. Rather, they were organizational visionaries. They created a constitution and focused on building a country. In essence they

54

were governance architects and engineers. In reality, they were builders of what Carver (1997) called cybernetic awareness, which is defined as drawing focus naturally to the harmony of the whole.

Chait, Holland, and Taylor (1996) argued that renewal and re-engineering of nonprofit governance begins with the president and board chairperson creating the forums and activating the procedures for board members to discuss the board's effectiveness and to discover whether concerns about the board's performance are widespread or limited (p. 23). In short, board development must be championed by an individual, such as the president or board chairperson, who is generally perceived to have the legitimacy to act. Nevertheless, Schein (1993) asserted that organizational participants are unlikely to accept that current modes of operation are inadequate and ineffective without "intense communication", usually by the group's leaders, of "discomforting data ... any items of information that show the organization that some of its goals are not being met or that some of its processes are not accomplishing what they are supposed to" (p. 299). The learning moment here appears to be that intense communication by the president or board chairperson about issues of consequence, such as governance effectiveness, makes the need for change within the board more overt and more imperative.

The shared leadership linkage between the need for governance reform and the champion(s) of the processes is found within the concept of servant leadership. Covey (2004), an internationally respected leadership authority, in his book, *The 8th Habit – From Effectiveness to Greatness*, emphasized:

55

That when the spirit of servant leadership takes hold in a team, and between a manager or team and an associate … trust ensues and it is this trust that is shared and reciprocated between the members of the group – it is this trust that is the essence of how a person becomes the leader of their boss. (p. 261)

In support of this proposition, Warren Bennis (1989), in his now famous book, *On Becoming a Leader*, identified, "vision, inspiration, empathy, and trustworthiness" as the key characteristics of effective leaders (p. 140). As well, a number of noted leadership authors have looked at issues of a leader's character. James Hillman (1996), in *The Soul's Code: In Search of Character and Calling*, described the "invisible source of personal consistency, for which some use the word habit; psychology today calls character and character refers to deep structures of personality that are particularly resistant to change" (p. 260).

It is identified that the terms servant and leader are usually thought of as being opposites. Even though the term servant leadership is paradoxical in nature, many of today's most creative thinkers in the fields of governance and management, such as Warren Bennis, John Carver, Stephen Covey, M. Scott Peck, Peter Senge, and Margaret Wheatley, to name a few, herald the idea as the emerging leadership paradigm. In her groundbreaking book on quantum sciences and leadership, *Rewriting the Corporate Brain*, Zohar (1997) punctuated the point and stated that, "servant leadership is the essence of quantum thinking and quantum leadership" (p. 146).

Hence, if shared leadership is to become a reality, it would appear that it is the champion(s) of the renewal and the re-engineering processes that must first change and accept their role as a servant-leader. This appears to be the first factor associated with improving board governance efficiency. It is the letting go of hierarchical-based structures and traditional power centres in higher education institutions, which is a conscious choice for the champion(s). The upside to that choice is found with Robert K. Greenleaf (1977), in his book, *The Servant as Leader*, who says that the best test of servant leadership is found in the answers to the following three questions: (1) do those served grow as persons, (2) do they, while being served, become healthier, wiser, freer, more autonomous, more likely themselves to become servants, and (3) what is the effect on the least privileged in society; will they benefit, or, at least, not be further deprived (p. 266)?

The Three Remaining Factors

Having explored shared leadership through the challenges associated with re-engineering board governance processes and the need for servant leadership on the part of the champion(s) of the processes, it is timely to review the three remaining factors seen to be associated with the improvement of board efficiency. In doing so, the review will examine the effects of the following: (1) board member human capital composition, (2) governance-related education and training of board members, and (3) the board's view of themselves as stewards and listeners to the voice of the college.

This discussion will begin by examining what is considered to be improved board efficiency. Chait, Holland, and Taylor (1996) found that there are six specific behaviors or competency sets that distinguish strong boards from weak boards. In short, an effective board demonstrates a capacity in six dimensions. They are as follows:

1. Contextual – understands the culture and values of the organization it governs.
2. Educational – well-informed about the organization, their roles, responsibilities, and performance.
3. Interpersonal – creates a sense of the board members as a group, fostering inclusiveness and teamwork.
4. Analytical – recognizes the complexities of issues and uses multiple perspectives to develop appropriate responses.
5. Political – accepts the need to develop and maintain healthy relationships among key constituencies.
6. Strategic – develops a vision for the organization and helps ensure a strategic approach to the future.

Carver (1997) took things a step beyond competencies and specific behaviors, which distinguished effective boards, and suggested some techniques, or policy development considerations that aid in maintaining an improved governance system. They are as follows:

1. Board member recruitment;
2. Board member orientation;
3. Board self-evaluation; and
4. Education.

Jay W. Lorsch, in his Harvard Business Review (2000) Corporate Governance essay, *Empowering the Board*, added to the discussion of improved board effectiveness and efficiency from the perspective of the board – CEO relationship. He stated:

> What is required is a new form of teamwork in which board members and top-level managers understand one another's roles and responsibilities and collaborate effectively to achieve [corporate] success. This scenario, however, means that the CEO must understand clearly the power and responsibility of the board and board members must recognize and respect the boundary between monitoring management and actually managing the organization. (p. 27)

This new form of teamwork, which necessitates a collaborative approach to board governance, is a foundation component of shared leadership.

Factor Two – Board Human Capital Composition or Mix

Historically, board members were selected because of social, economic, and political standing. Additionally, their politeness and ability to get along with others were normally taken into consideration. Mace (1971) described [board] directors as "ornaments" on the corporate Christmas tree (p. 99). Unfortunately, for the ornaments of yesteryear, today's complex governance setting demands multi-dimensional and talented individuals to perform the role of board members.

Nevertheless, as Caroline Oliver pointed out, in *The Policy Governance Fieldbook* (1999), "in most cases new board members come from the traditions of management rather than governance, of hands-on involvement rather than policy involvement, and sometimes, of supporting a particular constituency rather than working for the ownership as a whole" (p. 172). Hence, a human resource problem-in-the-making unfolds should there not be positive interventions in the recruitment, orientation, and training areas.

Generally speaking, as explained by Chait, Ryan, and Taylor (2005), "a board contributes various types of [human] capital, and then invests those resources in the governance of the institution. In the best cases, the capital represented by the board appreciates substantially over time. The boards with the most capital provide the organization with a comparative edge and the ability to 'out govern' the competition" (p. 139).

One of the meanings of shared leadership means working together in complex, real-world situations. Additionally, if the relationship between the board and senior administration is more like a partnership, than a 'we-they' situation, it is reasonable to assume, as presented by Moxley (2002), that there is more vitality and spirit experienced weaving individuals and their relationships. However, it is important to note that partnership in teams is effective when leadership happens as a team of people working to accomplish a shared goal. Unfortunately, this shared leadership state is not possible unless, as Chait, Ryan, and Taylor (1996) posited, "board members and senior staff must learn to recognize, appreciate, and capture the value of four, no less, crucial forms of (human) capital, beyond money, that board members can provide. These are intellectual, reputational, political, and social capital" (p. 139). In support of shared leadership, and the recognition of the importance of human capital, Smith (2006) weighed in and offered up the need for the development of board member skills, such as team building, conflict management, and the building of a new culture.

Factor Three - Governance-related Education and Training

Carver (1997) expressed that [governance] excellence can be lost through the arrival of new [board] members who have not engaged in the process of improvement. In fact, as they bring their own expectations from other settings, the potential exists for them to cause a regression. Carver insisted that orientation should be mandatory; as it is crucial the new members learn the principles of board governance as soon as possible so that they may make meaningful contributions.

Chait, Holland, and Taylor (1996) presented a strong case for the need for governors to become well informed, particularly about the inner workings as opposed to just reviewing the financial statements of the institution. The researchers identified the characteristics of the most successful and ongoing education programs, which include elements such as mutually orchestrated professional development opportunities by administrators and governors. Other opportunities include education and training clearly targeted to the governor's role and the provision of access and dialogue with key stakeholders and constituencies.

However, according to Davis (1997), the most common professional development topic is budget and financial management. The second most common topic is the board member's role and responsibilities, and then the board-president relationship. Be that as it may, Davis (1997) suggested that the president can take a proactive role in professional development planning and encourage the board orientation and development. Davis (1997) posited that a good professional development program nurtures board member development in six areas. They are as follows: (1) appreciation of the college's context or history and current setting, (2) curiosity and an appetite for board member education, (3) familiarity with effective group process techniques, (4) inclination to engage in step-by-step and logical analysis, (5) interest in communicating with key college constituencies, and (6) appreciation of strategic plans.

Garfield's (2004) proposition was that the community college governance environment has become increasingly legalistic, which has caused the board's work to evolve into much more complex and challenging domains. He noted several examples of these highly legalistic impacts on governance responsibilities including such areas as: (1) rights of individual board members, (2) internal board relations, (3) external board relations, (4) board member liability, (5) conflicts of interest, (6) conduct at public meetings, (7) public records issues, and (8) board member financial responsibilities. Even though Garfield may have been correct in asserting the importance of legal education and training for board members, it should be noted that shared leadership is considered pluralistic, dynamic, and requires a broader worldview, which is strategic and generative in nature.

It was purported by the National Governors Association (2001) that policymakers should be vigilant in ensuring that the governing boards of large or growing institutions have the scale, skill mix, and institutional memory required to oversee the increasingly complex higher education institutions. This article was indicative of a growing trend in North America towards legislating basic education and training for board members. In this regard, one of the proposed long-term values of this study may be to provide insight(s) relative to the need and design of education and training programs necessary for boards, who practice shared leadership and, who seek improved efficiency.

Factor Four - Stewardship and Listeners to the College's Voice

Firstly, stewardship is not normally related to ownership; rather, it is related to nurturing and giving back something in better condition than it was given to you. Indigenous cultures clearly see the ancient and fixed link between land [place] and humans. In this regard, Leilani Holmes, in Sefa Dei, Hall, and Rosenberg (2002), when referencing Hawaiian culture, said, "actually nobody owns the land ... trees, air, water, and everything that gives life are [again] described as subjects who must be approached in the right way, who must be asked, and who must be respected" (p.45).

Similarly, it may be reasonable to assert that governance, nor shared leadership, is not really about ownership – it is about representing the interests of the owners, and perhaps more importantly, it is about stewardship, and about approaching the college in the 'right way,' with respect. It may be about a sincere ability to listen to its voice.

Pulitzer prize winning author Dr. Robert Coles (2000) noted the late Senator Robert Kennedy saying, "you learn what's ahead through the living of it – what to do, the same way" (p.39). Upon reflection of the Senator's comments, Coles (2000) offered these comments:

> The living of it – I kept hearing in my head: the living of leadership, the living of an effort to do some good in this world, and prompt others to follow along; the living of it as exemplified by someone who had done lots of living in his forty-three years, and who, at that time, had less than twelve months left of his life to enjoy (p.39).

The living of leadership is characterized, as well, by Bolman and Deal (1995), noted authors of *Reframing Organizations,* in their powerful and best-selling story, *Leading With Soul.* Their primary character was a beleaguered executive, who sought purpose and passion after listening intently to the voice of his spiritual guide. He confessed, "She taught me that leading is giving. That spirit is the core of life. [She] helped me find my soul ... together we are finding our company's soul. We're building an uncommon spirit. One seed. Many plants, a shared dream" (p.137).

In relation to 'good leadership', John Wooden, considered by many one of the greatest coaches in the history of college basketball, stressed in Johnson (2003), that "one does not try to be a leader. ... One that is deeply and vitally concerned with those under his leadership and one that is interested in finding about the best way to accomplish things rather than having his own way" (p.187). Relative to teamwork, Wooden offered, in Johnson (2003), "the best way to improve the team is to improve ourselves" (p.182).

Building upon Wooden's teamwork concept, James MacGregor Burns (1978), in *Leadership,* his Pulitzer Prize and National Book Award winning book, when commenting upon effective leadership in the collective state explained,

> As followers respond [to the leader], a symbiotic relationship develops that binds leader and follower together into a social and political collectivity. Cadres form; hierarchies evolve; structure hardens. Responding to leader's initiatives, followers address their hopes and demands to politicians who use their power resources relevant to those hopes and demands to satisfy them. Leaders seek to mobilize existing social collectivities, whether class, nationalistic, ethnic, or other (p.452).

With reference to small group conformity and the importance of goal-setting, Burns (1978) continued, "the standards of behavior with which group members are expected to comply are drawn from the explicit and implicit goals of the group ... group success and leader effectiveness are measured not only by the achievement of the task(s) but by the extent to which the task(s) embodies group values and the achievement furthers fundamental group goals" (p.295).

Closing Remarks

In December 2001, after three years of deepening recession and rising unemployment, Argentines marched, rioted, looted, and brought down their elected government. One half of the population was living in poverty, one quarter in destitution and children were dying of hunger. The country had five presidents in two weeks. At the height of this fatalism, some Argentines decided to try a new, more open approach. In short, they brought together hundreds of leaders from all parts of society in a series of roundtables, to talk about the crisis, to make proposals, and to act.

On the final morning of the workshop, after days of storytelling, listening, sharing, and converging, the group's conversations and ideas came together quickly. Team members announced initiatives that they wanted to spearhead and groups formed around these leaders to make plans. In essence, they were on their way towards a new reality.

What can we learn about shared leadership from this short story from Argentina, and from the preceding literature review? Perhaps it is this – a new reality in nonprofit governance may be needed and a meaningful change towards a new reality appears to be a challenge-rich environment. But, as asserted by Adam Kahane (2004), a world renown designer and facilitator of processes through which business, government, and civil society leaders learned to solve their toughest, most complex problems, "the common theme … is that the participants [need to be] able to sense, or remember, what the larger purpose was for their work and why it mattered to them individually and as a group – the sources of their shared commitment." He added, "in order to solve tough problems, we need more than shared new ideas. We also need shared commitment. We need a sense of the whole and what it demands of us" (p.103).

CHAPTER 3

RESEARCH METHODOLOGY

The purpose of this chapter is to describe the research methodology used for exploring the relationship between the practice of shared leadership and board effectiveness within the boards of the Western Canadian rural, public colleges. This study endeavored to identify and explain how does the practicing of shared leadership by a Western Canadian rural, public college board of governors affect their board effectiveness, and possibly their institution's performance. Secondly, this study sought to identify and explain what are the key factors, which appear to be associated with the practice of shared leadership and which have the most or least impact upon board effectiveness. What follows is a description of the design of the research, the instrumentation, the data collection, and the data analysis used for exploring these relationships.

Research Design

The research was characterized by the selection and adoption of a variety of inquiry methodologies based upon a mixed method research perspective. The study was researched primarily from an epistemology of objectivism. Crotty (2003) defined objectivism as, "the epistemological view that things exist as meaningful entities independently of consciousness and experience, that they have truth and meaning residing in them as objects" (p.5). Thus, this study sought to conduct careful research that attained objective truth and meaning, understanding that the research process itself, was the researcher's primary justification. As Crotty (2003) claimed, "expounding the research process, including the assumptions or propositions the researcher brings to the methodology, assumes obvious importance" (p.42).

In this mixed method research study, shared leadership was examined using a variety of instrumentation. The purpose of using a different variety of instrumentation is for triangulation. Triangulation is the use of different methods to research the same issue to increase the reliability of the results.

In this study, data were collected via semi-structured interviews, documentary analysis, and a survey questionnaire to board members. Conducting the semi-structured interviews and completing the documentary analysis, prior to the construction and administration of the survey questionnaire, was central to the use of mixed methods in an integrated and sequenced way. It was recognized that the way in which the methodologies were sequenced and combined made a difference in the process of conducting the study and in the results. Furthermore, it was noted that making decisions about how best to sequence and combine methods depended on the nature of this inquiry and was a matter of judgment and experience.

The overall inquiry purpose of this mixed method study was exploratory. The intent of the investigative inquiry was to explore the relationship between the practice of shared leadership and board effectiveness within the boards of the rural, public colleges. The inquiry was centered on a number of informed factors that were expressed in a way which could be tested. Essentially, the objective of the deductive study was to focus on the possible relationship between two or more factors, associated with the practice of shared leadership, by a rural, public board and to assess their effect upon improving board effectiveness.

In terms of instrumentation and data collection, the researcher sought to design and use quantitative based methods and instruments. As well, with reference to the study's data analysis and inference(s), the researcher sought to place the emphasis on measurement when collecting and analyzing data.

Instrumentation

The board chairperson and president visits utilized a semi-structured interview instrument, whereupon responses were recorded to allow for coding in the analysis phase of the research. In addition, each of the eight institution's board secretaries were surveyed and asked to provide key information, artifacts, and documents. This information was intended to provide a comparative guide for the institutions, as well as quantitative measures data against which qualitative assessments could be made institution to institution. To complement this mixed method study, the research included the administration of the survey questionnaire, which was forwarded electronically to all 11 board members in each of the eight participating institutions.

Board members, including presidents and board chairpersons, were sent formal documents on the investigation, including an agreement to have their institution included in the study and a copy of the interview consent form used later in on-site interviews. This package and covering letter was forwarded under the signature of the researcher, who explained the study and assured confidential treatment of responses.

Prior to site visits, semi-structured interview questions were developed and pilot tested, with one current president and one former board chairperson, as well as the study advisor, for clarity, completeness, and brevity. Pilot testing occurred at sites that were not a part of the investigation. Questions were both specific and open-ended and invited the presidents and board chairpersons to explain and elaborate on their responses. Participants' responses were recorded and coded. The data were analyzed primarily from an epistemology of objectivism. The integrated approach utilized the interpretive methodology of survey research using an ethnographic questionnaire. The document sources requested included government documents pertaining to performance envelope awards, and institutional documents pertaining to annual reports, presidential search, board orientation manuals, board policy manuals, multi-year board approved business plans, and professional development workshops agendas, along with supporting materials.

Following the completion of the semi-structured interviews, and the collected documents and artifacts, the data were used in the development of the survey questionnaire. This development utilized the analytical framework of Chait, Holland, and Taylor (1996). This framework delineated six competency sets inherent in effective boards. This framework was developed by Chait, Holland, and Taylor (1996) after visits to 22 campuses, interviews with more than 110 trustees and college presidents, and self-assessment survey responses from over 400 board members. Questions in the survey questionnaire were categorized by board governance behaviors that contributed to the practice of shared leadership.

The competency sets are as follows:

1. Contextual Dimension
2. Educational Dimension
3. Interpersonal Dimension
4. Analytical Dimension
5. Political Dimension
6. Strategic Dimension

The closed questions of the survey questionnaire were developed and pilot tested for clarity, completeness, and brevity with one sitting president and one sitting board chairperson, as well as the study advisor. Pilot testing of the survey questionnaire occurred at a participating site following the completion of the semi-structured interviews.

The survey questionnaire contained 38 questions addressing the following variables: (1) shared leadership understanding, (2) practicing shared leadership, (3) focus on institutional performance, (4) president's governance-related knowledge, skills, and abilities associated with the board's practice of shared leadership and board governance efficiency, (5) board's competencies which underscore board governance efficiency, (6) board's human capital, and (7) community commitment to life-long learning [or not] may be a reflection of the board's governance-related work.

For over 20 years, electronic mail has been used to distribute survey questionnaires and to collect data from research participants. For example, in 1986 the results from the first e-mail survey were published in Public Opinion Quarterly (Kiesler & Sproull, 1986). Generally speaking, e-mail surveys have demonstrated superiority over other distribution modes of surveys in terms of response speed and cost efficiency.

For the purposes of this study, an e-mail distribution mode provided for a more immediate means of response (Flaherty, et al., 1998) as compared to direct mail. In addition, e-mail has the potential to provide heightened response quality. Respondents to an e-mail survey tend to be more candid than responses to mail or phone surveys (Bachman, Elfrink & Venzana, 1999). The literature supported that multiple follow-ups, typically yield higher response rates versus one-time reminders (Heberlein & Baumgartner, 1978). For this reason, three weekly reminders, each including the original survey questionnaire, were forwarded to all board members who had not responded to date. A general trend of declining average response rates that use e-mail to collect data was noted by Sheehan (2001), as having a 15% drop between 1995/6 (46%) and 1998/9 (31%). The average response rate of this questionnaire, however, was 55.7% and considered to be above average.

The survey questionnaire was prepared to test and measure the relationship between the practice of shared leadership and board effectiveness. Face validity, as defined by Wikipedia (2007), is a property of a test intended to measure something. A test is said to have face validity if it "looks like" it is going to measure what it is supposed to measure.

The survey questionnaire was prepared to measure the variables, as outlined in the five research questions. Prior to the administration of the questionnaire, a sitting board chairperson and president were consulted, and both agreed that overall the instrument's questions looked like a valid test of the variables which may be associated with the practice of shared leadership and board effectiveness.

In summary, the exploration of the relationship between the practice of shared leadership and board effectiveness benefited from the blending of a positivist and constructivist theoretical perspective. Specifically, the positivist perspective informed the constructivist perspective in that the responses derived from the semi-structured interviews were used to inform the construction of the survey questionnaire. Given the unabashed input(s) received during the semi-structured interviews by the eight board chairpersons and presidents [i.e. experts], the construction of the survey questionnaire was informed and served to support the claim of face validity of instrument's questions as a valid test of the variables.

Data Collection

The 16 semi-structured interviews were completed by April 2007. All interviews took place at the eight Western Canadian rural, public colleges. There were two key respondents per institution (involving both the president and board chairperson). The eight institutions were selected because they represented nearly 90% of the entire sample of the sector.

The researcher was familiar with all participants, and thus, site access was not contested. The study focused on the eight rural, public colleges to generate new theory on the effects on board effectiveness by boards, which practiced shared leadership, in a non-metro setting.

The researcher was a participant observer throughout all semi-structured interviews. The interview was used to encourage the respondents to discuss their views regarding what extent their board practice did shared leadership and what was the extent of the four factors, as identified in the literature, deemed essential for board effectiveness. As well, participants offered views on what extent boards understood the concepts of shared leadership, what extent the institution's performance reflected the board's practice of shared leadership, and what extent did the larger community's higher education awareness, participation, and attainment reflect the board's practice of shared leadership. Each semi-structured, recorded interview was approximately one hour in duration and involved open-ended questions. Glesne (1999) considered the purpose of such interviewing is "to capture the unseen that was, is, will be, or should be: how respondents think or feel about something; and how they explain or account for something" (p.93).

The survey questionnaire was administered electronically in May 2007 at the eight rural, public colleges to the eleven board members. In each college, the board included the chairperson, president, six publicly appointed members, one faculty representative, one staff representative, and one student representative. Gorard (2001) explained that the use of a survey is indicated when the data required does not already exist and the research questions are not susceptible to experimental trial for practical reasons, such as lack of resources or ethical constraints. The reader will recall that the survey questionnaire was sequenced to follow the semi-structured interviews, such that the survey's design could be informed by the interviews. It included an introduction, a few questions about the respondent, a number of substantive questions, and background questions.

The study of the multiple sites in depth through semi-structured interviews, survey questionnaires and document analysis, provided multiple viewpoints. These served to confirm and disconfirm preliminary propositions, all contributing to a richer and more accurate exploration of the sites.

Board members, including presidents and board chairpersons, were sent formal documents on the investigation, including an agreement to have their institution included in the study and a copy of the interview consent form. This package and covering letter was forwarded under the signature of the Olds

College President, who explained the study and assured confidential treatment of responses.

Semi-structured interview questions were specific and open-ended and invited the presidents and board chairpersons to elaborate on their responses. Their responses were recorded. The researcher reviewed and analyzed the data collected at each site and prepared a detailed report.

The document sources, which were collected from the board secretaries, included government documents pertaining to performance envelope awards, and institutional documents such as annual reports, presidential search and board orientation manuals. As well, they included board policy manuals, multi-year board approved business plans, and professional development workshops agendas, with supporting materials.

All 11 board members in the eight institutions were forwarded via e-mail the survey questionnaire and requested to complete it using a word document and return it to the researcher via e-mail within 14 days of the receipt of the questionnaire. In an effort to increase the response rate, once every week an electronic follow-up reminder was sent to each board member.

Data Analysis

On a college by college basis, all responses from the 16 semi-structured interviews were recorded and transcribed. Then, the data were coded and analyzed. The content analysis of the data included counting of coded data by category and the identification and explanation of specific themes such as: (1)

shared leadership, (2) institutional performance, (3) human capital, (4) stewardship, (5) board effectiveness, and (6) governance modes of thinking and working together relative to the community's commitment to life-long learning.

In the case of two institutions, to probe their alignment with policy-based governance, institutional documentary data and artifacts underwent further analysis according to source or type – policies, business plans, performance data – and were coded using a modified pattern of shared leadership categories, as developed by Chait, Ryan, and Taylor (2005). This pattern described three modes of governance as leadership. They are as follows:

1. Fiduciary mode
2. Strategic mode
3. Generative mode

After coding, content analysis of the data included counting of coded data by category and the identification and explanation of specific themes. Thematic analysis led to a clearer understanding of the meaning of the patterns.

The data from the questionnaires were received within one month of the first mailing. It was then entered into a database in CoStat version 6.311, by Cohort Inc., Monterey, California. Analytical parameters included descriptive statistics and correlations. Descriptive statistics data were mean, standard deviation, sum of values, minimum value, maximum and number of values (n).

Once the data were entered, institutional mean values for the parameters were used to derive the Pearson Product Moment correlation coefficient values. The Pearson Product Moment Correlation Coefficient ('r') is a measure of the linear association of two independent variables. Hence, if the probability that 'r' = 0 ['P(r = 0)'] is <=0.05, 'r' is significantly different from 0 and the variables show some degree of correlation. Therefore, a very strong correlation (P<0.05) is obtained when -0.7200>r>0.7200.

To summarize, it is emphasized that this study used a triangulation approach through interviews, survey questionnaire, and documentary analysis in the case of two institutions. The coding and analysis of the data were connected to shared leadership behaviors and to the modes of thinking and working together as a board.

CHAPTER 4

THE ANALYSIS AND INTERPRETATION OF THE RESEARCH

Introduction

The purpose of this chapter is to present the results of the mixed research methods deployed to explore the relationship between the practice of shared leadership and board effectiveness within the boards of rural and publicly funded Western Canadian colleges. In this chapter, the results and the analysis of the mixed methods are presented sequentially, beginning with the eight sets of semi-structured interviews, followed by an analysis of the documentation and artifacts comparing two of the colleges in depth and concluding with the results and the analysis of the system- wide survey questionnaire.

Semi-structured Interviews

The semi-structured interview accounts that follow are grouped within the context of the college in which they were conducted. Structuring the multiple units of analysis, in this manner, suggested some patterns, connections, and disconnections among the participant's responses in each college.

The semi-structured interviews were conducted from March 2007 to April 2007 at the eight rural and publicly funded Western Canadian colleges with two key participants – the board chairperson and president. Why were the board chair and president selected as the two key participants in the semi-structured interviews? Chait, Holland, and Taylor (1996) asked board members – from their Trustee Demonstration Project sites – what advice they would offer to another board about how to improve. The preponderance of their responses emphasized the role of leadership. They stated, "Start at the top. Are your board chair and president capable, skilled, and committed to improve? If not, make change first there. You better have good leadership. There's no substitute for it" (p.79).

Participants were provided with the interview questions at least two weeks in advance of the interview. Upon arrival at their institution, the researcher obtained written consent from each of the participants. For the purpose of anonymity, each participant was provided with the opportunity to select their own name, or pseudonym, by which they would be known in the study. Each participant was interviewed individually and all comments were tape recorded, subsequently transcribed, coded, and analyzed.

The responses of the Board Chairs and Presidents to the questions were evaluated and coded to reflect the comparative degree of contribution and effectiveness. High, medium, and low levels of contribution and effectiveness were coded 3, 2 and 1 respectively. The coded data were used to calculate the extent to which the board practiced shared leadership and the effectiveness of the board, as seen in Tables 1- 9. Typical responses and levels of effectiveness are shown below.

Level	Typical Responses
High	Superlatives such as: • Excellent • Very good • Very often • Uppermost • Key role • Extremely important • Very distinctive • Very significant • Very large • Extensive • Any other positive superlative or elative description that denotes very high level of contribution or involvement
Medium	Descriptions of activities, contributions or involvement that denote acceptable level, such as: • Good • Significant • Fairly good • Fairly key role • Any other qualitative descriptions with positive but not superlative connotation
Low	Responses such as: • Very limited • Sporadic • Sometimes • Rarely • Minimal involvement • Fair • Other descriptions or connotations that represent or infer low on unacceptable level

In exact order of interviewing, the eight colleges are numbered and abbreviated as follows: (1) IONE, (2) ITWO, (3) ITHREE, (4) IFOUR, (5) IFIVE, (6) ISIX, (7) ISEVEN, and (8) IEIGHT.

Institution One [IONE]

Overall, the IONE board chair (c), known in this study as Cow Boss, appeared to be prepared and provided 'to the point' responses to the questions. In contrast, the IONE president (p), known in this study as Norton, appeared to be prepared, however provided responses which seemed illusive.

Cow Boss has served two terms as a board member – the last two years as the board chair. Presently, Norton is one of the longest serving presidents in the Alberta postsecondary system.

The questions, noteworthy responses, and comments follow:

Extent of understanding exhibited by your board to the practice of shared leadership

Both participants demonstrated a very good understanding of the shared leadership concept and concurred that the board demonstrates their understanding of the same, by focusing on policy development and institutional performance. According to Cow Boss:

> That is where I see our board sort of focuses on its strength. We work very closely with the president in developing policy and institutional performance, president's performance, mostly monitoring president's evaluation but also through reporting by the president at the meetings as far as institutional performance and where we are at, and where we are going. (P001-5)

Extent to which your board practices shared leadership

Again, both participants appeared to be in unison – this time in their concurrence relative to the board always practicing shared leadership. Both participants focused their comments on the shared leadership practice of democratic processes, honesty, and shared ethics – that which seeks a common good rather than secrecy, deception, and politics.

Extent that the institution's performance reflects your board's practice of shared leadership

Cow Boss agreed with the concept that the institution's performance is a reflection of the board's practice of shared leadership and demonstrated a high reflection level in his response, offering that the employment rate of graduates is an indicator of the board's practice. As well, Norton agreed and demonstrated a very high reflection in his response and cited incremental enrolment growth initially, as an indicator of the board's practice of shared leadership. He added that enterprise revenue generation is also an indicator of the board's practice. Norton added:

> We also pride ourselves on the entrepreneurial side of the college and, some years ago, we contracted out our cafeteria service and that served us well. We actually make money on our cafeteria. We have a Starbucks on campus. We make money with that too. But again, that is done with a private business person who comes on campus and operates those kinds of services for us and the board sees that as an important aspect of who we are. (P002-7)

Extent of the contribution of the president's governance competency and performance associated with the board's practice of shared leadership and effectiveness

Cow Boss agreed with the concept that the president's governance competency is a critical factor associated with the practice of shared leadership and effectiveness. He offered comments which reflected a very high contribution level. Norton agreed with the concept, as well; however, his comments reflected a medium contribution level. Additionally, Cow Boss said:

> The competency and performance of the president are key to shared leadership. The board has faith in the president's ability that he can go ahead and do his job, follow the strategic plan, the business plan, and the budget – probably the three key documents that the board uses to guide the President – and stays within the limitations that are laid out in the policy for the president. (P001-8)

Extent of the contribution of the board's human capital composition associated with their practice of shared leadership and effectiveness

Cow Boss agreed with the concept that the board's human capital composition is a critical factor associated with the practice of shared leadership and effectiveness. According to him:

> The human capital composition of the board is what makes a board. I don't know what the right term is but, its different people from different walks of life, different experiences; all the uniqueness that they bring to the board (P001-10).

In fact, he offered comments which reflected a very high contribution level. Norton did not agree with the concept and offered comments which reflected a low contribution level. Regarding the human capital, Norton said, "I have learned over the years not to take anything to the board that I think I am going to lose so I'll generally go with things that I think I am going to win" (P002-13).

Extent of the contribution of the board's governance-related education and training associated with their practice of shared leadership and effectiveness

Both participants concurred with the concept that the board's education and training is associated with the practice of shared leadership and effectiveness. However, each offered comments at the medium contribution level.

Extent of the contribution of the board's view of themselves as stewards and listeners to the college's voice associated with their practice of shared leadership and effectiveness

Cow Boss agreed with the concept that the board's view of themselves as stewards and listeners to the college's voice is a critical factor associated with the practice of shared leadership and effectiveness. In fact, he offered comments which reflected a very high contribution level. Norton did not agree with the concept and offered comments which reflected a low contribution level. For example, while Cow Boss stated: "We make a strong effort to listen to the community, and our stakeholders ... and share that with the president" (P001-14), Norton's view is, "We try to encourage everyone to talk to everyone. Right now it is a good time within the province so there's not a lot of bitching or aggravation that is going on" (P002-14).

> *One or two examples that would illustrate the external community's commitment and capacity to embrace life-long learning and which would reflect the extent to which your board works in all three governance as leadership modes – fiduciary, strategic, and generative*

Cow Boss focused on the business and industry community and offered two examples of the external community's commitment and capacity to embrace life-long learning. He suggested that the recruitment of employees and new businesses could be considered a function of the board working in all three governance as leadership modes. Likewise, Norton agreed with the concept and suggested that the college's advisory committees, fundraising activities, and the use of college facilities by community groups and organizations, were examples of the same.

Patterns, Connections, and Disconnections

Based upon the responses of the board chair and president, as noted in Table 1, it would appear that the practice of shared leadership does exist within the board. Both respondents agreed that the practice of shared leadership does significantly affect their board's effectiveness. Likewise, both respondents agreed that the practice of shared leadership does affect their institution's performance.

However, some disagreement did exist between the board chair and president regarding what key factors are associated with their practice of shared leadership. Whereas, the board chair was convinced that the factors including the president's governance competency, the human capital composition of the board, the board's view of themselves as stewards and listeners to the college's voice, are very high contributors to the board's practice of shared leadership, the president was less convinced. In fact, he argued that the president's governance competency is of only medium contribution to the board's practice of shared leadership. As well, the president was pointed in his assessment of the contribution of the human capital composition of the board and the board's view of themselves as stewards and listeners, as he assigned both factors to the low contribution level. Lastly, both participants agreed and assigned a medium contribution level to the board's governance-related education and training factor associated with their practice of shared leadership and efficiency.

In summary, based upon an assessment of the degree of alignment of the competencies model of Chait, Holland and Taylor (1996), with the reflections and contributions, provided by the board chair and the president, it would appear that IONE may be deemed to have a very effective governing board, as seen in Table 9 (p.136).

Overall, the IONE board appears to understand the culture and norms of the organization it governs. They tend to ensure that the board members are knowledgeable about the institution and the board's role, responsibilities, and performance. To some degree, the board seems to create a sense of inclusiveness among the board members. The board tends to approach matters from a broad institutional outlook and respects the need to develop and maintain healthy relationships among major constituencies. Overall, the board organizes itself and conducts its business in light of the institution's strategic priorities.

TABLE 1

Summary of IONE Board Chair (C) and President (P) Responses Demonstrating the Relationship of Contribution Levels with the Dimensional Analysis by Chait, Holland, and Taylor (1996) and the Board's Practice of Shared Leadership

		Low	Medium	High
Contextual	C			X
	P			X
Educational	C		X	
	P		X	
Interpersonal	C			X
	P	X		
Analytical	C			X
	P	X		
Political	C			X
	P	X		
Strategic	C			X
	P		X	

Institution Two [ITWO]

Overall, the ITWO chair, known in this study as Wheat from Chaff, appeared to focus his responses on what an ideal board should do, as opposed to what his board actually does. In fact, Wheat from Chaff did not seem to be very focused on the questions, but rather chose to exert his influence and offer his own opinions and commentary. For instance, on several occasions he indicated that his leadership goal for the board was to have them informed, engaged, and responsible, yet his comments did not seem to support the theoretical ideal. On another occasion, he submitted that the governance objective was to be more collaborative versus contesting, more sharing versus dictatorial, yet, again, his commentary did not tend to profile such practices.

In contrast, the ITWO president, known in this study as Robert, appeared to be disconnected with his board, except for the board chair, with whom he has day to day contact. This is logistically possible as the board chair has an office within the college's executive suite. He commented:

> The board as a whole would have much more difficulty with that and, by and large, take things a lot more for granted, in which case, there is not near the extent of shared leadership at a board level, but with the board chair it's quite the opposite. At the board level, in general, with our current board, I think there is not the level of understanding. There may not be the time commitment necessary to truly understand the issue, although I do think there might be willingness. I am not sure I see the commitment for the board as a whole (Q002-2).

Wheat from Chaff is presently in his first term as both a board member and board chair. He was appointed about two years ago following an internal scandal, which resulted in the former president resigning and the former board chair being replaced. Robert is one of the newer presidents in the Alberta postsecondary system.

The questions, noteworthy responses, and comments follow:

Extent of understanding exhibited by your board to the practice of shared leadership

Wheat from Chaff demonstrated an adequate understanding of the shared leadership concept and offered as examples of the board's understanding of the same by the board's focus on policy development and institutional performance, along with the assurance that the mission of the college is achieved. In contrast, Robert demonstrated an adequate understanding of the shared leadership concept, as well, and offered as examples of the board's understanding regarding the complexity of the issues and its provision of proactive and visionary leadership. Wheat from Chaff said, "The one that caught my eye immediately was our focus on policy development. ... A few of the others, I could speak on them. We'll talk about the mission; ensure that the mission is achieved" (Q001-4). According to Robert:

> Okay, let's go on to the second one, 'provision of proactive and visioning leadership' and my comments would probably be similar to the last one, although the board would be more active in this one. In terms of deciding the future of the college and our general direction/vision – where we're going ten years from now, the board was involved in the process and certainly involved in the final decision making, but perhaps not as much clarity as you would like to see. So, it almost became an approval process rather than a visioning exercise for them (Q002-4).

Extent to which your board practices shared leadership

Wheat from Chaff indicated that the board often practiced shared leadership citing as his example, the quality of the board members' interactions. However, Robert disagreed and offered that the board never practiced shared leadership. Robert suggested that the practice of shared leadership was a direct function of meetings between the board chair and he. However, in attempting to provide evidence of the practice of shared leadership during meetings, he indicated that there is very little communication between board members by offering:

> Other than the board chair, there is very little in the way of communication with the balance of the board members. I would say that shared leadership is not exemplified by our board either through conversational or formal communication - particularly not conversational (Q002-5).

Extent that the institution's performance reflects your board's practice of shared leadership

Wheat from Chaff agreed with the concept that the institution's performance is a reflection of the board's practice of shared leadership and demonstrated a high reflection level in his response offering that the employment rate of graduates is an indicator of the board's practice. Within the context of the board, Robert disagreed with the concept and demonstrated a no reflection level in his response. According to him, "That is not really, or has not really been dealt with at the board level – didn't even get on the radar screen" (Q002-7). However, he suggested that incremental enrolment growth would certainly be an indicator if the practice of shared leadership existed.

Extent of the contribution of the president's governance competency and performance associated with the board's practice of shared leadership and effectiveness

Wheat from Chaff agreed with the concept that the president's governance competency is a critical factor associated with the practice of shared leadership and effectiveness. According to him, "The board's number one decision, the most important decision a board will make is the hiring of the CEO, the President" (Q001-8). He offered comments which reflected a very high contribution level. Robert agreed with the concept, as well; however, his comments reflected a medium contribution level. The comments addressed the function of an ideal CEO and not the role and function of the president at ITWO.

Extent of the contribution of the board's human capital composition associated with their practice of shared leadership and effectiveness

Wheat from Chaff agreed with the concept that the board's human capital composition is a critical factor associated with the practice of shared leadership and effectiveness. In fact, he offered comments which reflected a very high contribution level. According to Wheat from Chaff:

> I think it's a critical point. As we recruit people for key executive positions, likewise boards need to recruit people for board positions to bring to the board table a range of talent, a range of backgrounds, a range of abilities. (Q001-5)

Robert did not agree with the concept and offered comments which reflected a low contribution level:

In terms of the expertise of dealing with complicated issues, the large organization issues, I think that in rural Alberta, probably most rural areas of Canada, maybe North America, that it is difficult to find people that have the kind of experienced background. … So I think the human capital side of the board is a bit of an issue here (Q002-6).

Extent of the contribution of the board's governance-related education and training associated with their practice of shared leadership and effectiveness

Wheat from Chaff concurred with the concept that the board's education and training is associated with the practice of shared leadership and effectiveness. However he offered comments at the medium contribution level. According Wheat from Chaff , "All of those things, I think they are essential. In terms of formal training, personally, I sometimes look at some of these things with a bit of jaundiced eye" (Q001-7). Robert did not agree with the concept and offered comments relative to the board's governance-related education and training at the no contribution level. According to Robert, "It's sporadic. In terms of what I'll call formal professional development for board members or board's training in governance, there's not a lot" (Q002-7).

Extent of the contribution of the board's view of themselves as stewards and listeners to the college's voice associated with their practice of shared leadership and effectiveness

Wheat from Chaff agreed with the concept that the board's view of themselves as stewards and listeners to the college's voice is a critical factor associated with the practice of shared leadership and effectiveness. In fact, he offered comments at a very high contribution level. He said, "That's extremely important, and we talk a bit about that as this college developed its new mission, vision and values and I think that would be a classic case of shared leadership" (Q001-8). However, Robert did not agreed with the concept and offered comments at the low contribution level. Robert said, "I think that the board does do that in a very narrow focus. I'm not sure they do it in a very broad perspective" (Q002-8).

> *One or two examples that would illustrate the external community's commitment and capacity to embrace life-long learning and which would reflect the extent to which your board works in all three governance as leadership modes – fiduciary, strategic, and generative*

As his two examples of the external community's commitment and capacity to embrace life-long learning, and symbolic of the board's ability to work in all three governance as leadership modes, Wheat from Chaff focused on the idea(s) that the college was the largest employer in the area and was considered by many to be the centre of the community. As his example, Robert noted that the college is often the venue for major public events, whereupon the college is indirectly promoted to various government and business entities.

Patterns, Connections, and Disconnections

Based upon the responses of the board chair and president, as noted in Table 2, it would appear that the practice of shared leadership exists in theory, but not to any significant degree in practice within the board. Even though the respondents agreed that the understanding of shared leadership is shared by board members, the respondents appeared to disagree regarding the practice of the same by the board. Likewise, there is disagreement between the respondents regarding the practice of shared leadership significantly affecting their institution's performance.

Their comments suggested a less than effective board environment with limited communication between board members. The board cannot be characterized as united, or as an entity which discusses and debates the key issues. Robert's comments suggest a high degree of micro management practices, particularly by the board chair. There is little to no evidence of strategic or generative thinking by the board, as many key decisions are made during informal discussions between the board chair and the president, which happen outside the formal board meetings. In short, Wheat from Chaff indicated that the former board was used by the former president as a rubber stamp mechanism for major decisions and this got the institution into trouble. Consequently there have been major changes and Wheat from Chaff is convinced that he was brought in by government to 'fix it.'

Moderate to significant disagreement exists between the board chair and the president on several different factors which include the following: (1) extent to which the board practices shared leadership, (2) extent to which the institution's performance reflects the board's practice of shared leadership, (3) extent of the contribution of the president's governance competency, (4) extent of the contribution of the board's human capital composition, (5) extent of the contribution of the board's governance-related education and training, and (6) extent of the contribution of the board's view of themselves as stewards and listeners to the college's voice.

In summary, based upon an assessment of the degree of alignment of the competencies model of Chait, Holland and Taylor (1996), with the reflections and contributions provided by the board chair and the president, it would appear that ITWO may be deemed to have a less effective governing board, as noted in Table 9 (p.136).

Overall, outside of the board chair and the president, the ITWO board does not appear to understand the culture and norms of the organization it governs. The leaders, particularly the board chair, tend to ensure that the board members are 'kept in the dark' about the institution and the board's role, responsibilities, and performance. There is little to no evidence of the board creating a sense of inclusiveness amongst the board members. The board chair and the president, only, tend to approach matters from an institutional outlook and appear to respect the need to develop and maintain healthy relationships among major constituencies. Overall, the board does not seem to organize itself and conduct its business at the strategic or generative levels of working together, or in light of the college's priorities.

TABLE 2

Summary of ITWO Board Chair (C) and President (P) Responses Demonstrating the Relationship of Contribution Levels with the Dimensional Analysis by Chait, Holland, and Taylor (1996) and the Board's Practice of Shared Leadership

		Low	Medium	High
Contextual	C	X		
	P	X		
Educational	C		X	
	P	X		
Interpersonal	C			X
	P	X		
Analytical	C			X
	P		X	
Political	C		X	
	P	X		
Strategic	C			X
	P		X	

Institution Three [ITHREE]

The ITHREE board chair, known in this study as Harley, appeared to be busy and in several cases did not respond to the questions directly. However, Harley was direct in his belief that the college was inextricably linked to the community and that one of their primary responsibilities was community development, which included the sectors of services, arts, skilled labour, and health and wellness.

In contrast, the ITHREE president, known in this study as Zippy, appeared to be poised and responded to the questions in a concise and to the point fashion.

Harley, a respected businessman in the community, is in his first term and first year as the board chair. However, he served two terms as a board member in the past. Zippy was hired about four years ago following the firing of the president, who had served only nine months in the position.

The questions, noteworthy responses, and comments follow:

Extent of understanding exhibited by your board to the practice of shared leadership

Both participants demonstrated a very good understanding of the shared leadership concept and concurred that the board demonstrates their understanding of the same by focusing externally. As well, the president indicated that the board demonstrates their understanding via their focus on policy development and institutional performance. According to Zippy:

> The other area, on policy development and institutional performance, certainly reflects the notion that the board sets overall policy but that we mutually work on that appropriate policy and then look at what we expect for institutional performance (R002-2).

Extent to which your board practices shared leadership

Both participants agreed that the board practices shared leadership. Harley offered his concurrence at the often practiced level citing the board's value for democratic processes, honesty, and shared ethics – that which seeks a common good rather than secrecy, deception, and politics. Zippy submitted his concurrence at the usually practiced level citing the quality of the board members' interactions, as opposed to interaction by position, and similar to Harley, the board's value for democratic processes, honesty, and shared ethics.

Extent that the institution's performance reflects your board's practice of shared leadership

Harley agreed with the concept that the institution's performance is a reflection of the board's practice of shared leadership and demonstrated a medium reflection level in his response offering as examples the employment rate of graduates and the college's enterprise revenue generation. Zippy agreed with the concept, as well; however, demonstrated a very high reflection level in his response offering the same examples as the board chair.

Extent of the contribution of the president's governance competency and performance associated with the board's practice of shared leadership and effectiveness

Both participants agreed with the concept that the president's governance competency is a key factor associated with the practice of shared leadership and effectiveness. Harley offered comments which reflected a very high contribution level, whereas Zippy's comments reflected a high contribution level. Harley said:

> Certainly we have really excellent leadership in our president and in terms of his involvement in the community and recognizing what his job is in terms of dealing with industry in the

community, this type of thing, our president has done a really good job (R001-6).

Extent of the contribution of the board's human capital composition associated with their practice of shared leadership and effectiveness

Both participants agreed with the concept that the board's human capital composition is a key factor associated with the practice of shared leadership and effectiveness. They both offered comments which reflected a high contribution level. According to Harley, "The diversity and the expertise of those individuals around the board really is very positive" (R001-7), and Zippy added, "We strategically try to have board members appointed that fit the strategic interests of the college" (R002-7).

Extent of the contribution of the board's governance-related education and training associated with their practice of shared leadership and effectiveness

Harley concurred with the concept that the board's education and training is associated with the practice of shared leadership and effectiveness, however, offered his comments at the medium contribution level. He said, "We do and I think that at our annual board retreat, we often focus on it. Especially for new board members coming on to the board, it's important" (R001-8). Zippy did not agree with the concept and offered his comments at the low contribution level. According to him, "We certainly periodically focus the board on governance matters. ... We put some effort into that. I would say that we will have a major focus on policy governance not annually, but periodically" (R002-8).

Extent of the contribution of the board's view of themselves as stewards and listeners to the college's voice associated with their practice of shared leadership and effectiveness

Both participants agreed with the concept that the board's view of themselves as stewards and listeners to the college's voice is a key factor associated with the practice of shared leadership and effectiveness. Harley submitted his remarks at the medium contribution level, while Zippy registered his comments at the high contribution level. According to Harley, "The diversity of our board and being a small community that we're in.... I think all of those people, I guess, bring feedback to the board table" (R001-9). Zippy said, "I think there is a very good understanding of the stewardship role" (R002-9).

One or two examples that would illustrate the external community's commitment and capacity to embrace life-long learning and which would reflect the extent to which your board works in all three governance as leadership modes – fiduciary, strategic, and generative

Both participants cited the college's involvement with regional communities and work with major industries such as the oil sands as examples of the external community's commitment and capacity to embrace life-long learning. As well, the participants suggested that the examples could be construed to represent the extent to which the board works in all three governance as leadership modes.

Patterns, Connections, and Disconnections

Based upon the responses of the board chair and the president, as seen in Table 3, it would appear that the practice of shared leadership does exist within the board. Both respondents agreed that the practice of shared leadership does affect their board's effectiveness. Likewise, both respondents agreed that the practice of shared leadership does affect their institution's performance.

In general, agreement exists between the participants regarding the contribution of several key factors associated with their practice of shared leadership. They agree on the following factors: (1) extent of the contribution of the president's governance competency, (2) extent of the contribution of the board's human capital composition, and (3) extent of the contribution of the board's view of themselves as stewards and listeners to the college's voice. However, disagreement does exist between the board chair and the president regarding the extent of the contribution of the board's governance-related education and training. By his comments, it would appear that the chair is moderately disposed in his support for the education and training variable, whereas, the president is adamant in his comments that the factor provides no contribution to the development of shared leadership and effectiveness.

In summary, based upon an assessment of the degree of alignment of the competencies model of Chait, Holland and Taylor (1996), with the reflections and contributions provided by the board chair and the president, it would appear that ITHREE may be deemed to have a very effective governing board, as seen in Table 9 (p.136).

Overall, the ITHREE board relies on the college's mission, values, and tradition as a guide for decision-making. The board tends to regularly seek information and feedback from their publics on its own performance. Leadership is cultivated within the board and the institution. The board seeks to approach matters from a broad institutional and community outlook and consults often and communicates directly with key constituencies. Lastly, it would appear that the board organizes itself and conducts its business in light of the college's strategic priorities.

TABLE 3

Summary of ITHREE Board Chair (C) and President (P) Responses Demonstrating the Relationship of Contribution Levels with the Dimensional Analysis by Chait, Holland, and Taylor (1996) and the Board's Practice of Shared Leadership

		Low	Medium	High
Contextual	C		X	
	P			X
Educational	C		X	
	P	X		
Interpersonal	C			X
	P			X
Analytical	C			X
	P			X
Political	C			X
	P			X
Strategic	C			X
	P			X

Institution Four – [IFOUR]

Overall, the IFOUR board chair, known in this study as Marci, appeared to be less than engaged. Perhaps, the reason was related to the timing of the interview. It occurred on a Friday afternoon shortly following a visit to the College by the new Premier of the province and a couple of hours prior to the community's annual citizen of the year dinner. In contrast, the IFOUR president, known in this study as Lee, appeared to be guarded, yet knowledgeable, regarding policy governance, partnerships, and shared leadership.

Marci has served nearly two terms as a board member – the last two years as board chair. Lee is one of the newer presidents in the Alberta postsecondary system, having come to the position from a vice president posting at a community college abroad.

The questions, noteworthy responses, and comments follow:

Extent of understanding exhibited by your board to the practice of shared leadership

Both participants demonstrated an adequate understanding of shared leadership and concurred that the board demonstrates the same by shaping institutional direction. According to Marci:

> We have worked with our new president to develop more of a practice of shared leadership in that the board is now trying to focus more on the values area and the bigger picture of where we are going and less on approving particular pieces of budget or smaller administrative kind of areas (T001-2).

Additionally, Marci cited another example of the board demonstrating their understanding by the quality of the board members' interactions versus interaction by position. As well, Lee offered another example of the board demonstrating their understanding by virtue of the board's ensuring of continuous learning.

Extent to which your board practices shared leadership

Again, both participants appeared to be in unison – this time in their concurrence relative to the board always practicing shared leadership. Marci's response reflected a usually practices level of concurrence, while Lee's response reflected an always practices level. Marci's example of practicing was focused on how board members think and work together when in a problem solving mode, whereas Lee's examples of practicing were focused firstly on the board's communication which is considered conversational rather than formal, and their value for democratic processes, honesty, and shared ethics, which seeks a common good rather than secrecy, deception, and politics.

Extent that the institution's performance reflects your board's practice of shared leadership

Once again, both participants appeared to be of the same mind – this time in their concurrence relative to the extent that the institution's performance reflects the board's practice of shared leadership. Marci's response reflected a high reflection level of concurrence, while Lee's response reflected a very high level. Both participants cited the employment rate of graduates as an example of the institutional performance reflecting the board's shared leadership practices. Additionally, Marci offered administrative expenses as a percentage of overall college expenses as another example, while Lee submitted graduate satisfaction as her second example of the same.

Extent of the contribution of the president's governance competency and performance associated with the board's practice of shared leadership and effectiveness

Marci disagreed with the proposition offering comments at the low contribution level, whereas Lee agreed with the concept that the president's governance competency is a critical factor associated with the practice of shared leadership and effectiveness and submitted comments at a very high contribution level. According to Lee:

> I think it's very much been a partnership between the board and me in terms of changing the way that we work together and changing the role of what the board does, as compared to what it used to do (T002-5).

Extent of the contribution of the board's human capital composition associated with their practice of shared leadership and effectiveness

Generally, both participants agreed with the concept that the board's human capital composition is a factor associated with the practice of shared leadership and effectiveness. Marci's comments reflected a high contribution level of concurrence, while Lee's sentiments reflected a medium contribution level of agreement.

Extent of the contribution of the board's governance-related education and training associated with their practice of shared leadership and effectiveness

Both participants were adamant about the concept that the board's education and training is essential and associated with the practice of shared leadership and effectiveness. In support of this factor, both participants offered comments at the very high contribution level.

Extent of the contribution of the board's view of themselves as stewards and listeners to the college's voice associated with their practice of shared leadership and effectiveness

Both participants agreed with the concept that the board's view of themselves as stewards and listeners to the college's voice is a factor associated with the practice of shared leadership and effectiveness. However, they tended to differ in the degree of their concurrence. Marci offered sentiments at the medium contribution level, while Lee submitted comments at the very high contribution level. According to Lee, "You're responsible to your owners. I like to say stakeholders. The government owns us in principle, I guess, but it's the stakeholders, the people in southern Alberta that have an interest in what we do" (T002-9).

One or two examples that would illustrate the external community's commitment and capacity to embrace life-long learning and which would reflect the extent to which your board works in all three governance as leadership modes – fiduciary, strategic, and generative

In this regard, the board chair's comments were focused on the board's involvement in the community in fundraising for a new college building, along with ongoing discussion with the regional health region about their new facility. The president's comments were centered on the college's goal of becoming a higher education leader in the sustainability and renewable energy sector.

Patterns, Connections and Disconnections

Based upon the responses of Marci and Lee, as noted in Table 4, it would appear that the practice of shared leadership does exist within the board. Both respondents agreed that the practice of shared leadership does affect their board's effectiveness. Likewise, both the chair and the president concurred that the practice of shared leadership does affect their institution's performance.

General agreement existed between the chair and the president regarding the extent of the contribution of several key factors considered to have an impact on shared leadership and effectiveness. They include the human capital composition of the board, the governance-related education and training of the board, and the board's view of themselves as stewards and listeners to the college's voice.

However, disagreement does exist between the board chair and president regarding the extent of the contribution of the president's governance competency and performance associated with the board's practice of shared leadership and effectiveness. Whereas the president is convinced that the president's governance competency is a very high contributor to the effort, the board chair is less convinced offering her comments at a low contribution level.

In summary, based upon an assessment of the degree of alignment of the competencies model of Chait, Holland and Taylor (1996), with the reflections and contributions, provided by the board chair and the president, it would appear that IFOUR may be deemed to have an effective governing board, as seen in Table 9 (p.136).

Generally, the IFOUR board seems to take into account the culture and the norms of the college it governs. They value and take the necessary steps to ensure that board members are knowledgeable about the college and their roles, responsibilities, and performance. The board appears to nurture the development of board members as a working group and they seem to recognize the complexities and subtleties of issues and ambiguities, approaching challenges from a broad institutional outlook. The board chair and president appear to respect the integrity of the political processes and the roles of the various stakeholders. Lastly, there is evidence to suggest that the board helps the college envision a direction and shape various strategies.

TABLE 4

Summary of IFOUR Board Chair (C) and President (P) Responses Demonstrating the Relationship of Contribution Levels with the Dimensional Analysis by Chait, Holland, and Taylor (1996) and the Board's Practice of Shared Leadership

		Low	Medium	High
Contextual	C			X
	P			X
Educational	C			X
	P			X
Interpersonal	C			X
	P		X	
Analytical	C		X	
	P			X
Political	C			X
	P		X	
Strategic	C	X		
	P			X

Institution Five [IFIVE]

The IFIVE board chair, known in this study as The Old Guy, is a respected businessman in his community and a recognized CEO in the provincial circles. He is known as a student of policy governance having worked with sophisticated policy governance models within the ranks of his own board. The Old Guy is in his second term as a board member having spent the past three years as board chair. Likewise, the president, known in this study as Sherbrook, is a seasoned and respected CEO in the system. He has spent nearly a decade in his executive position and responded to the questions in a straight to the point manner. Along with his various board chairs, it would appear that Sherbrook has significantly contributed to the development of a culture of trust within the board of governors. Both participants appeared to be gracious, accommodating, and focused on the concept of shared leadership during the course of the interviews.

The questions, noteworthy responses, and comments follow:

Extent of understanding exhibited by your board to the practice of shared leadership

Both participants exhibited a very good understanding of the shared leadership concept and concurred that the board demonstrates their understanding of the same by focusing externally. As well, the president added that the board focuses on policy development and institutional performance; whereas, The Old Guy added that the board demonstrates their understanding by their comprehension of the issues.

Extent to which your board practices shared leadership

Both participants agreed that the board always practices shared leadership. The board chair cited as his example the independence of all board members and their ability to be active in the leadership process rather than defer to distinct differences between leaders and followers. Sherbrook noted two different examples. One – the quality of the board members' interactions rather than interactions by position, and two – the board's value for democratic processes, honesty, and shared ethics, which seeks a common good rather than secrecy, deception, and politics. In Sherbrook's words, "Both the quality of their interactions and how they work together is really critical in their concept of shared leadership" (U002-3).

Extent that the institution's performance reflects your board's practice of shared leadership

Both participants concurred with the notion that the institution's performance is a reflection of the board's practice of shared leadership. Similarly, they agreed in offering the examples of the employment rate of graduates and graduate satisfaction. However, they seemed to differ in opinion as to the degree of reflection. The Old Guy demonstrated a medium reflection level in his responses; whereas, Sherbrook demonstrated a very high reflection level within his comments.

Extent of the contribution of the president's governance competency and performance associated with the board's practice of shared leadership and effectiveness

Both participants agreed with the idea that the president's governance competency is a key factor associated with the practice of shared leadership and effectiveness. Their comments reflected a very high contribution level. For example, The Old Guy said:

> He gives us that guidance and there is a very distinct air of trust between us, and I think I alluded to it a little bit earlier, that we trust each other and the practice of shared leadership and efficiency, so far as the president's contribution is, I believe, providing us a level of comfort and guidance that we know we don't have to question and that we know that we trust him and it's there. (U001-4)

Extent of the contribution of the board's human capital composition associated with their practice of shared leadership and effectiveness

Both participants agreed with the notion that the board's human capital composition is a key factor associated with the practice of shared leadership and effectiveness. For example, according to Sherbrook:

> I would say in our case, it is very, very large in the sense that our board actually has a policy that outlines how they will, in fact, recommend the selection of new member, so when they get people on the board, they come with set of perspectives and skills to the board (U002-6).

Their comments reflected a very high contribution level.

Extent of the contribution of the board's governance-related education and training associated with their practice of shared leadership and effectiveness

Both participants agreed with the concept that the board's education and training is a factor associated with the practice of shared leadership and effectiveness. Their comments reflected a high contribution level.

Extent of the contribution of the board's view of themselves as stewards and listeners to the college's voice associated with their practice of shared leadership and effectiveness

Both participants agreed with the idea that the board's view of themselves as stewards and listeners to the college's voice is a key factor associated with the practice of shared leadership and effectiveness. Their comments reflected a very high contribution level.

One or two examples that would illustrate the external community's commitment and capacity to embrace life-long learning and which would reflect the extent to which your board works in all three governance as leadership modes – fiduciary, strategic, and generative

Both participants suggested that the board does work in the strategic and generative modes and cited the following examples: (1) seniors' care facility built on the IFIVE campus, (2) integrated learning environment in a regional town, (3) community-wide fundraising initiative for the college information commons, and (4) community-wide involvement in the college arts centre.

Patterns, Connections, and Disconnections

Based upon the responses of The Old Guy and Sherbrook, as noted in Table 5, it would appear that the practice of shared leadership does exist within the board. Both respondents agreed that the practice of shared leadership does affect their board effectiveness. Likewise, both respondents agreed that the practice of shared leadership does affect their institution's performance.

Very strong agreement existed between the participants regarding the contribution of all four factors associated with the practice of shared leadership.

In summary, based upon an assessment of the degree of alignment of the competencies model of Chait, Holland and Taylor (1996), with the reflections and contributions provided by the board chair and the president, it would appear that IFIVE may be deemed to have a very effective governing board, as seen in Table 9 (p.136).

Overall, the IFIVE board seems to understand the culture and norms of the institution it governs. It appears to take the necessary steps to ensure that board members are knowledgeable and understand their roles and responsibilities. The board attempts to nurture the development of members as a working group by fostering a culture of trust and cohesiveness. It appears to recognize the subtleties of issues and has a relatively high tolerance for ambiguity. The board attempts to consistently develop and maintain healthy relationships among their major and minor constituencies. Lastly, they appear to facilitate the envisioning of a direction for the institution, along with shaping the various strategies required to attain the college vision.

TABLE 5

Summary of IFIVE Board Chair (C) and President (P) Responses Demonstrating the Relationship of Contribution Levels with the Dimensional Analysis by Chait, Holland, and Taylor (1996) and the Board's Practice of Shared Leadership

		Low	Medium	High
Contextual	C			X
	P			X
Educational	C			X
	P			X
Interpersonal	C			X
	P			X
Analytical	C			X
	P			X
Political	C			X
	P			X
Strategic	C			X
	P			X

Institution Six [ISIX]

The ISIX board chair, known in this study as Gordon, appeared to be busy; however, he maintained his focus during his interview. Similarly, the ISIX president, known in this study as Androgog, seemed to be prepared and rendered responses which were straight forward and direct.

Gordon, a respected local businessman, has been the chair for a little over a year. He appears to value higher education and policy governance. He was quick to indicate that the board is rich in terms of its human capital composition, with diverse representation ranging from the public to the private sector, along with multiple community memberships. Gordon emphasized the pride and the passion the board shows in their college, as well as their role as stewards. He emphasized the contribution that they make to the college and community(s) was very important. Additionally, it should be noted that the ISIX student population has a very high First Nations and Métis composition, which is a reflection of their northern and remote demographics.

The President, Androgog, is about three years from retirement having served in this executive position for the past seven years.

The questions, noteworthy responses, and comments follow:

Extent of understanding exhibited by your board to the practice of shared leadership

Both participants demonstrated a very good understanding of the shared leadership concept and concurred that the board demonstrates their understanding of the same by focusing on policy development and institutional performance. Gordon added one further example of their understanding by implying that the board seeks to provide proactive and visionary leadership, according to him, "We definitely are always evaluating if our mission statement is achieved. We demonstrate cohesiveness in seeking multiple perspectives" (W001-2).

Extent to which your board practices shared leadership

Both participants agreed that the board always practices shared leadership. As an example, Gordon intimated that the board tends to think and work together, as opposed to various problems being solved by a single leader. As his example, Androgog offered that the board's communication was conversational in nature versus formal.

Extent that the institution's performance reflects your board's practice of shared leadership

Both participants agreed with the concept that the institution's performance is a reflection of the board's practice of shared leadership and demonstrated a very high reflection level in their responses. Both participants offered enrolment growth as an example of the same and the board chair added graduate satisfaction as another example of the impact of shared leadership on institutional performance.

Extent of the contribution of the president's governance competency and performance associated with the board's practice of shared leadership and effectiveness

Both participants concurred with the concept that the president's governance competency is a key factor associated with the practice of shared leadership and effectiveness and offered their comments at the very high contribution level.

Extent of the contribution of the board's human capital composition associated with their practice of shared leadership and effectiveness

Both participants agreed with the concept that the board's human capital composition is a key factor associated with the practice of shared leadership and effectiveness and submitted their comments at the very high contribution level.

For example, Gordon said, "We have a very healthy, diverse mix of board members. Each of them bring their strengths" (W001-4).

Extent of the contribution of the board's governance-related education and training associated with their practice of shared leadership and effectiveness

Interestingly, there was not agreement with the notion that the board's education and training is associated with the practice of shared leadership and effectiveness. In fact, both participants offered their comments at the low contribution level. For example, pertaining to governance-related education, Andragog said, "We did it a few years ago. I think we might be ready for another dose of it" (W002-5).

Extent of the contribution of the board's view of themselves as stewards and listeners to the college's voice associated with their practice of shared leadership and effectiveness

Both participants agreed with the concept that the board's view of themselves as stewards and listeners to the college's voice is a key factor associated with the practice of shared leadership and effectiveness and offered their comments at the very high contribution level.

One or two examples that would illustrate the external community's commitment and capacity to embrace life-long learning and which would reflect the extent to which your board works in all three governance as leadership modes – fiduciary, strategic, and generative

Both participants emphasized that the college was the focus of the community and to some degree the region. As an example, both participants hastened to illustrate the same by speaking about their upcoming major sport entry into the Alberta Colleges Athletic Conference. The cost of operations, which are projected at $250,000.00, of this intercollegiate athletic program will be largely born by the business and industry sector of the community. Why? The community values their college and their sport, and sees this program development opportunity as a mutually beneficial initiative. The college will achieve additional enrolments, which they would not normally accrue, and the community will receive entertainment and community focus in return. Additionally, Gordon noted the community participation in the fundraising program associated with the development of the proposed one million dollar power engineering laboratory, along with the host community activities associated with the opening of a new campus of the college in a regional town.

Patterns, Connections, and Disconnections

Based upon the responses of Gordon and Androgog, as noted in Table 6, it would appear that the practice of shared leadership does exist with the board. Both respondents agreed that the practice of shared leadership does affect their board's effectiveness. As well, both respondents agreed that the practice of shared leadership does affect their institution's performance.

Very strong agreement existed between the two respondents regarding the contribution of three key factors associated with their practice of shared leadership: (1) extent of the contribution of the president's governance competency, (2) extent of the contribution of the board's human capital

120

composition and, (3) extent of the contribution of the board's view of themselves as stewards and listeners to the college's voice. Additionally, very strong agreement existed between the two respondents regarding the apparent lack of contribution of one factor associated with their practice of shared leadership such as the extent of the contribution of the board's governance-related education and training. Both respondents offered their comments of the same at the low contribution level.

In summary, based upon an assessment of the degree of alignment of the competencies model of Chait, Holland and Taylor (1996), with the reflections and contributions provided by the board chair and the president, it would appear that ISIX may be deemed to have a very effective governing board, as seen in Table 9 (p.136).

Overall, the board seems to understand the culture and norms of the college it governs. For the most part, they appear to take the necessary steps to ensure that board members are knowledgeable about the institution, and the board's roles and responsibilities. They appear to nurture the development of trustees as a working group and foster a sense of cohesiveness. They seem to recognize the complexities of internal and external issues and accept as a primary responsibility the need to develop and maintain healthy relationships among major constituencies including government. Lastly, the board appears to assist the institution to envision a set of directions and shape the associated strategies.

TABLE 6

Summary of IONE Board Chair (C) and President (P) Responses Demonstrating the Relationship of
Contribution Levels with the Dimensional Analysis by Chait, Holland, and Taylor (1996) and the
Board's Practice of Shared Leadership

		Low	Medium	High
Contextual	C			X
	P			X
Educational	C		X	
	P		X	
Interpersonal	C			X
	P		X	
Analytical	C			X
	P			X
Political	C			X
	P			X
Strategic	C			X
	P			X

Institution Seven [ISEVEN]

The ISEVEN board chair, known in this study as Trevor, was difficult
to access and on a couple of occasions postponed the appointment. The
ISEVEN president, known in this study as Golfer, appeared to be relaxed and
accommodating in his responses.

Trevor, a senior administrator in the public sector, who travels
extensively with his job, has been the board chair for close to one full term.
Early in the interview, he acknowledged the importance of shared leadership

122

as he believes it is an essential activity in empowering board members and the community. However, his responses indicated that his understanding of the idea was not consistent with the definition, but rather implied that his board preferred to defer most important decisions to their president. Golfer was in his third year as president having served the college in instructional and other administrative capacities for close to three decades. He acknowledged the importance of a holistic approach to governance particularly within an institution whose primary student population is of First Nations and Métis decent. He concurred with the board chair's notion that with full support, the board tends to defer those more important decisions and directions to the president.

The questions, noteworthy responses, and comments follow:

Extent of understanding exhibited by your board to the practice of shared leadership

Both participants demonstrated a working understanding of the shared leadership concept and agreed that the board demonstrates their understanding in various ways. For instance, Trevor's comments supporting the board demonstrating their understanding, reflected their focus on policy development and institutional performance, along with how they shape the institutional direction. As well, Golfer's comments reflected the board's understanding of the complexity of issues and their assurance that the mission of the college is achieved. According to Golfer:

> We've always felt that we're probably one of the strongest mission-driven organizations because of the clear role that our

board and our college see in working with communities. I think that the extent of their understanding around assuring the mission is achieved is very, very high (W002-1).

Extent to which your board practices shared leadership

Both participants agreed that the board always practices shared leadership and cited as an example the board's value for democratic processes, honesty, and shared ethics, which seeks a common good rather than secrecy, deception, and politics. As well, Trevor mentioned, as another example, the quality of the board's interactions. Additionally, Golfer noted, as another example, the way the board members think and work together rather than having the problems solved by the leader, only.

Extent that the institution's performance reflects your board's practice of shared leadership

Both participants agreed with the idea that the institution's performance is a reflection of the board's practice of shared leadership and gave the same two key performance indicators as examples. They are as follows: (1) employment rate of graduates, and (2) graduate satisfaction.

Extent of the contribution of the president's governance competency and performance associated with the board's practice of shared leadership and effectiveness

Both participants agreed with the notion that the president's governance competency is a key factor associated with the practice of shared leadership and effectiveness. The only differentiating element in their comments is that Golfer assigned the factor at the high contribution level, while Trevor assigned it at the very high contribution level.

Extent of the contribution of the board's human capital composition associated with their practice of shared leadership and effectiveness

Similar to the last factor, both participants concurred with the idea that the board's human capital contribution is a key factor associated with the practice of shared leadership and effectiveness. Again, the only differentiating element in their comments is that Golfer assigned the factor at the high contribution level, while Trevor assigned it at the very high contribution level. According to Trevor, "It's a good balance so the human capital composition is very well rounded and extremely important because it keeps balance within the governance structure. We are not lopsided or heavy on one end" (W001-4).

Extent of the contribution of the board's governance-related education and training associated with their practice of shared leadership and effectiveness

Both participants agreed with the concept that the board's education and training is associated with the practice of shared leadership and effectiveness, and offered their comments at the very high contribution level. Trevor referred to it as very key while Golfer rated it as, "Extremely high" (W002-5).

Extent of the contribution of the board's view of themselves as stewards and listeners to the college's voice associated with their practice of shared leadership and effectiveness

Both participants concurred with the idea that the board's view of themselves as stewards and listeners to the college's voice is a key factor associated with the practice of shared leadership and effectiveness, and supplied their comments at the very high contribution level.

One or two examples that would illustrate the external community's commitment and capacity to embrace life-long learning and which would reflect the extent to which your board works in all three governance as leadership modes – fiduciary, strategic, and generative

As his examples, Trevor noted the woodlands/forestry program and petroleum employment training program as evidence of the community's commitment to embrace life-long learning. As his examples of the board working in all three governance as leadership modes, Golfer offered the college's commitment to support northern and remote communities as community access points, and the ongoing inclusion of community cultural and celebratory events at the college.

Patterns, Connections, and Disconnections

Based upon the responses of Trevor and Golfer, as seen in Table 7, it would appear that the practice of shared leadership does exist to a degree with the board. Both respondents agreed that the practice of shared leadership does affect their board's effectiveness. Likewise, both respondents agreed that the practice of shared leadership does affect their institution's performance.

Generally, the respondents concurred regarding the extent of the contribution of all four key factors associated with the board's practice of shared leadership, and offered comments which reflected either a very high or high contribution.

In summary, based upon an assessment of the degree of alignment of the competencies model of Chait, Holland and Taylor (1996), with the responses provided by Trevor and Golfer, it would appear that ISEVEN may be deemed to have an effective governing board, as noted in Table 9 (p.136).

Overall, the board tends to take into account the norms of the college it governs and takes the necessary steps to ensure that members are knowledgeable about the college and the service region and the board's roles and responsibilities. Although there is a tendency to defer to the president for decisions and directions, they seem to nurture the development of members as a holistic working group and recognize the need to understand the complexities of the issues. The board appears to accept their responsibility to their many internal and external stakeholders and maintain healthy relationships amongst their major and minor constituencies. Lastly, in concert with their president, they tend to consistently assist their college in envisioning a direction and shaping the various strategies to get there.

TABLE 7

Summary of ISEVEN Board Chair (C) and President (P) Responses Demonstrating the Relationship of Contribution Levels with the Dimensional Analysis by Chait, Holland, and Taylor (1996) and the Board's Practice of Shared Leadership

		Low	Medium	High
Contextual	C			X
	P			X
Educational	C			X
	P			X
Interpersonal	C			X
	P			X
Analytical	C		X	
	P			X
Political	C			X
	P			X
Strategic	C			X
	P			X

Institution Eight [IEIGHT]

The IEIGHT board chair, known in this study as Country Boy, was generally off topic throughout the interview. However, it was clear from his input, that he was a student of policy governance and had done much reading in this regard. Country Boy admitted, early in the interview, that the board struggles with governance, as there is the continual tendency to focus on management and administrative issues.

128

In contrast, the IEIGHT acting president, known in this study as Taylor, was quite opinionated, knowledgeable relative to management issues, and to the point with his comments.

Country Boy, a respected businessman and volunteer in the community, is completing his second term as the board chair, with the past year clearly being the most traumatic, as the board had the unenviable task of terminating their president early in the academic session. Taylor, who retained his title as Vice President Academic over the past year, was hired about six years ago.

The questions, noteworthy responses, and comments follow:

Extent of understanding exhibited by your board to the practice of shared leadership

Both participants demonstrated an adequate understanding of the shared leadership concept and agreed that the board demonstrates their understanding of the same in a number of ways. As examples, Country Boy suggested the board's focus on policy development and institutional performance, along with how they shape the institutional direction. As well, Taylor offered that the board assures that the college mission is achieved and understands the complexity of the issues.

Extent to which your board practices shared leadership

Both participants concurred that the board practices shared leadership and offered as an example the board's demonstrated value for democratic processes, honesty, and shared ethics, which seeks a common good rather than secrecy, deception, and politics. As well, as another example Taylor submitted that the board's communication is conversational rather than formal.

Extent that the institution's performance reflects your board's practice of shared leadership

Country Boy agreed with the idea that the institution's performance is a reflection of the board's practice of shared leadership, however only demonstrated a medium reflection level in his comments and offered two examples in support of his agreement. They are as follows: (1) employment rate of graduates, and (2) enterprise revenue generation. Taylor was more emphatic within his comments, which were offered at the very high reflection level, and offered two examples, as well. They are as follows: (1) similar to Country Boy, employment rate of graduates, and (2) enrolment growth.

Extent of the contribution of the president's governance competency and performance associated with the board's practice of shared leadership and effectiveness

Both participants generally agreed with the notion that the president's governance competency is a key factor associated with the practice of shared leadership and effectiveness, however differed somewhat in the extent of the contribution. Country Boy offered comments which were at the high contribution level, while Taylor's comments reflected a medium contribution level.

Extent of the contribution of the board's human capital composition associated with their practice of shared leadership and effectiveness

Both participants concurred with the idea that the board's human capital composition is a key factor associated with the practice of shared leadership and effectiveness. They both offered comments which reflected a very high contribution level. For example, Country Boy said, "With the divergent opinions, you probably get more questions asked and you probably come up with better product at the end of the day" (S001-3). Taylor pointed out that, "When board positions become vacant, there's always a conversation about the human capital mix. There is an attempt to have aboriginal representations on our board" (S002-3).

Extent of the contribution of the board's governance-related education and training associated with their practice of shared leadership and effectiveness

Both participants agreed with the concept that the board's governance-related education and training is a key factor associated with their practice of shared leadership and effectiveness. They both offered comments which reflected a very high contribution level. Country Boy expressed, "I think a well-educated board that understands board governance and that communicates with each other is essential and it makes the college work a lot better" (S001-4).

Extent of the contribution of the board's view of themselves as stewards and listeners to the college's voice associated with their practice of shared leadership and effectiveness

Significant disagreement existed between County Boy and Taylor regarding this concept and its importance as a key factor associated with the board's practice of shared leadership and effectiveness. Whereas, Country Boy offered comments which indicated a low contribution level, Taylor was adamant in his remarks signaling a very high contribution level. In this regard, Taylor indicated a specific challenge exists as the board is often compromised in terms of whom to listen to and for what purpose, which tends to create tension within the ranks of the board.   While Country Boy said, "I believe that the board needs to know what's going on at the institution and they also need to know that they can question that" (S001-5), Taylor, said, "This board finds itself in a 'he said'-'she said' war of words between employee groups and the college administration" (S002-5).

One or two examples that would illustrate the external community's commitment and capacity to embrace life-long learning and which would reflect the extent to which your board works in all three governance as leadership modes – fiduciary, strategic, and generative

Country Boy struggled to offer examples citing only the board's commitment to deliver programs to the community within the college's mandate and their ability to work at the fiduciary level in the provision of an audit committee as per the recommendations of the auditor general of the province. Taylor indicated that the community's need for a skilled workforce was a college responsibility and in meeting that obligation the college contributes to the building of the community.

Patterns, Connections, and Disconnections

Based upon the responses of Country Boy and Taylor, as seen in Table 8, it would appear that the practice of shared leadership is a challenge and may only exist occasionally within the board. The board chair supported this proposition when indicating that there continues to be a misunderstanding within the ranks of the board as to their purpose. For example, there are some members who believe that the primary purpose of the board is that of a 'watchdog' over administration, while others see their responsibility as policy makers, fiduciary responsibility officials, and external relationship builders. Nevertheless, both respondents concurred that the practice of shared leadership does affect the board's effectiveness. Likewise, both respondents agreed that the practice of shared leadership does affect their institution's performance.

In general terms, agreement existed between Country Boy and Taylor regarding the extent of the contribution of three of the four key factors associated with the board's practice of shared leadership and effectiveness. However, as was noted earlier, they disagreed strongly on the fourth factor – the board's view of themselves as stewards and listeners to the college's voice – which may have indicated some of the residual fall-out effect associated with the termination of the president in the past year.

In summary, based upon an assessment of the degree of alignment of the competencies model of Chait, Holland and Taylor (1996), with the reflections and contributions provided by the Country Boy and Taylor, it would appear that IEIGHT may be deemed to have a less than effective governing board, as noted in Table 9 (p.136).

From the evidence, it would appear that the board struggles on occasion to take into account the culture and norms of the organization it governs. Similarly, the board is challenged to take the necessary steps to ensure that members are knowledgeable about their college, their region, and specifically, their roles and responsibilities as board members. The board tends to nurture the development of members as a working group, however struggles with a sense of inclusiveness amongst the board members. The board is challenged to understand the complexities of the issues, as they are many times looking at the management implications versus the governance implications of a particular issue.

After the termination of their president, they continued to struggle with accepting their responsibility to develop and maintain healthy relationships with their major and minor stakeholders. Lastly, it is certainly not clear from the data that this board assists the institution in a consistent fashion in envisioning a direction or in the provision of macro level strategies for the accomplishment of the same.

TABLE 8

Summary of IEIGHT Board Chair (C) and President (P) Responses Demonstrating the Relationship of Contribution Levels with the Dimensional Analysis by Chait, Holland, and Taylor (1996) and the Board's Practice of Shared Leadership

		Low	Medium	High
Contextual	C		X	
	P		X	
Educational	C		X	
	P		X	
Interpersonal	C			X
	P			X
Analytical	C		X	
	P			X
Political	C	X		
	P			X
Strategic	C	X		
	P		X	

135

TABLE 9

All Boards Summary of Board Effectiveness [i.e. based on the dimensional analysis by Chait, Holland, and Taylor (1996) and the maximum points for each dimension]

	IONE	ITWO	ITHREE	IFOUR	IFIVE	ISIX	ISEVEN	IEIGHT
Contextual (3)	3	1	2	3	3	3	3	2
Education (3)	2	2	3	3	3	2	3	2
Interpersonal (3)	2	3	3	2	3	3	2	3
Analytical (3)	3	2	3	3	3	3	2	2
Political (3)	3	2	3	2	3	3	3	2
Strategy (4)	4	2	3	3	3	3	3	2
	17/19	12/19	17/19	16/19	18/19	17/19	16/19	13/19
Effectiveness	89%	63%	89%	84%	95%	89%	84%	68%
	High	Low	High	Medium	High	High	Medium	Low

Note: The points awarded are based on the number of attributes identified from the responses of the Board Chair and President in the Non-Structured Interview. Effectiveness is rated High $\geq$ 85%, Medium $\leq$ 85%, and Low $\leq$ 70%

Document and Artifact Analysis

Upon completion of the semi-structured interviews at each of the eight colleges, between March 2007 to April 2007, and to better understand governance processes, the board secretaries, as requested, provided key information, artifacts, and documents. The document sources included government documents pertaining to the institution's 2004-2005 and 2005-2006 performance envelope awards, as well as various documents such as annual reports, presidential search, orientation manuals, policy manuals, professional development workshop agendas, and other supporting artifacts.

Focusing specifically on only two comprehensive community-based college governance boards – one less effective [ITWO] and one very effective [IFIVE], as defined previously in the analysis of the semi-structured interviews – their board's processes and performance were analyzed according to source or type using common documents and artifacts.

One of the common documents chosen for analysis was the 2006-2010 business plan. The Ministry of Advanced Education and Technology mandates the submission annually of a board approved four-year business plan document. Even though a college's business plan may include many other value-added sections, the Ministry provides a standard template for all institutions outlining what sections are mandatory. For example, in terms of the mandated business plan lay-out, all plans should address sections such as: (1) institutional context, (2) opportunities and challenges, (3) strategic plan, (4) accessibility plan, (5) enrolment plan, (6) financial plan, and (7) capital project development plan and resources required. Consistent with the analysis of the semi-structured interviews, the business plan data from both colleges was analyzed using the analytical framework of Chait, Holland and Taylor (1996).

The second set of common documents chosen for analysis was the board policies of each of the two colleges. The province's Auditor General mandates the development and maintenance of board policies by each of the public college boards. Again, even though a board's policy manual may include many value-added governance sections, there are sections that are expected by the Auditor General such as the college mandate, values, mission, and vision. The board policies underwent a second coding and analysis according to source and type and were coded using a modified pattern of shared leadership categories, as developed by Chait, Ryan and Taylor (2005), which outlined the three modes of governance as leadership. They are as follows: (1) fiduciary, (2) strategic, and (3) generative.

The third set of common documents and artifacts chosen for analysis was the Ministry of Advanced Education and Technology performance measures. This institution performance instrumentation, developed by the Ministry of Advanced Education (2006), annually identifies five key performance indicators, which are tracked and aggregated into a performance envelope scorecard, which is used to provide an incentive for certain behaviors and to award incremental revenues to higher performing institutions. Over the past 10 years, these key performance indicators have reflected three specific ministerial outcomes. They are as follows: (1) responsiveness, (2) accessibility, and (3) affordability. Correspondingly, the indicators for responsiveness include employment rate of graduates and graduate satisfaction. Accessibility is a stand-alone indicator and measures incremental enrolment growth using a three year rolling average. Lastly, affordability is measured using two indicators, which are administrative expenses as a function of overall expenses and the amount of enterprise revenue generated.

Business Plan(s) Analysis

Introduction

As suggested, the Ministry's business plan expectation of the college is to detail how the organization expects to move from current circumstances to their preferred state during the next four years. Generally, this articulation requires a nonprofit board to extrapolate how it intends to move from the present to the future. Normally, people, policies, programs, incentives, budgets, and facilities are harmonized within the plan. Hopefully, the plan specifies what changes must be made to the basic organizational structure and development of new or renovated programs, facilities, and services, to accommodate the intended set of goals. Once received, the Ministry reviews, comments, and begins to integrate certain elements of the various institution's plans into their own four-year business plan, which in theory becomes a part of the government's business plan and budget for the upcoming year.

In theory, as indicated by Chait, Ryan and Taylor (2005), plans should reflect strategic thinking more than strategic planning. They stated:

Wisdom, knowledge, and experience are widely distributed in an organization, thus a transformative idea can spring from anywhere. Strategic thinking occurs as a democratic process, not in the sense that everyone votes and the majority wins, but rather that everyone has opportunities to champion a point of view and to exert influence based on the quality of one's ideas rather than one's place on the organization chart (pp.64-65).

Consequently, for the purpose of this analysis, it is suggested that a college's business plan reflected the organization's strategies, rested on new concepts and reconsidered value propositions, received board discussion and debate, and that the president and/or board chair were not the sole source(s) of these ideas.

ITWO Business Plan

From a contextual and political dimensions perspective the college's 2006-2010 business plan (2006) complied with the ministerial directed guidelines. Evidence existed to support the basic areas required in a business plan, which included the institutional context, opportunities and challenges, the strategic plan, accessibility, enrolment, and financial plans, and capital project development plans complete with the outline of needed resources.

Foundationally, the board approved business plan was silent from an educational and interpersonal dimensions perspective, as there was no indication how the board's ends statements – values, vision, mission, and outcomes – may have reflected vigorous debate relative to the proposed strategies, as outlined in their various sub-plans. In fact, there was no mention whatsoever in the plan of the board's ends statements. This condition is consistent with semi-structured interview data, where in one instance Robert suggested, "that the (board) practice of shared leadership was a direct function of meetings between the board chair and himself."

From an analytical and strategical dimensions perspective, there appeared to be significant gaps in the college business plan regarding the development of the academic plan and the strategic enrolment management plan. Specifically, with a focus on academic planning for example, there was no indication of curriculum renewal, capacity building, and innovations in program delivery, learner success strategies, and advisory board linkages. As well, with a focus on strategic enrolment management for instance, there was no indication of retention strategies, learner success, recruitment strategies, admissions, applied research, marketing and communication activities, and database management. This vacuum may be consistent with the semi-structured interview findings whereupon Robert's comments suggested a high degree of micro management practices, particularly by the board chair. As well, as stated in the semi-structured interview analysis, both participants' comments reflected little to no evidence of strategic or generative thinking by the board, as many key decisions are made during informal discussions between the board chair and the president – most of which occur outside of the regularly scheduled board meetings.

Similar to the semi-structured interview findings, which posited the ITWO board as less effective, it would appear that their business plan data supported a very limited worldview of organizational development focused at the fiduciary level of planning. This data, which is embedded in various

141

quotes, appeared to be attributable to the president, who in concert with the board chair, is expected to present to the board all solutions to knotty problems.

Understanding that the province of Alberta has been providing a six per cent incremental increase to the base operating grant(s), along with several other financial funding packages during the past three years; the following statements found in the business plan (2006) of ITWO may represent the board's limited perspective to organizational planning and design. They are offered as follows:

1. The cost of offering cutting-edge technological training is escalating at a rate much faster than the college's ability to fund the technology.
2. Access funding continues to be the best way for [non-metro] colleges to expand their core programming.
3. The cost pressures are significant including negotiated agreements, facility maintenance and repairs, technology upgrades, program equipment, system upgrades, professional development and other factors ..... It challenges the college to control its costs.
4. Opportunities come in all shapes and forms. However, given the scarcity of resources, not all opportunities can be pursued.

Lastly, although their business plan represented the 2006-2010 planning cycle, the projected revenues to support the plan were reflective of the 2004-2005 fiscal year rather than 2005-2006 and as illustrated in Figure 1.0.

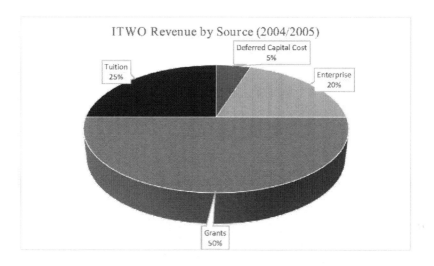

Figure 1.0 - ITWO 2006-2010 Business Plan – i.e. revenue by source

IFIVE Business Plan

From a contextual and political dimensions perspective the college's 2006-2010 business plan (2006) complied with the ministerial directed guidelines. Evidence existed to support the basic areas required in a business plan, which included the institutional context, opportunities and challenges, the strategic plan, accessibility, enrolment, and financial plans, and capital project development plans complete with the outline of needed resources.

Relative to the educational and interpersonal dimensions perspective, the college's business plan articulated the mandate and ends statements of the board of governors, which included their values, vision, mission, and outcomes. The plan suggested that the various proposed strategies were

143

reflective of a values-based orientation of the board. This orientation suggested that the board has taken the necessary steps to ensure that members are knowledgeable about the college, the service area, and their roles, responsibilities, and performance. Clearly, these ends-related sections reflected the college's commitment to exceeding the basic expectations of government and stakeholders, which is symbolic of stewardship. These reflections are consistent with the structured interview findings, whereupon review of the comments of The Old Guy and Sherbrook, which reflected a high contribution level, both agreed with the idea that the board's view of themselves as stewards and listeners to the college's voice was a key variable associated with the practice of shared leadership and [board] effectiveness.

The analytical and strategical dimensions of an effective governing board illustrate institutional leadership and are well represented in the plan by the well aligned commentary associated with the college's various sub-strategies. An example of the same included an academic strategic plan, complete with tactics associated with curriculum renewal and development, innovative program delivery, learner success, and institutional capacity building. Another example of a value-added, and shared leadership, set of strategies included a strategic enrolment management plan, inclusive of actions, targets, measures, and critical timelines for the development of sub-plans associated with retention, student success, conversion processes, marketing, applied research, and credit program enrolment goals. This distinction was not surprising given the data uncovered in the semi-structured interviews, where upon The Old Guy indicated that the IFIVE board always practiced shared leadership and cited as his example, the independence of all board members and their ability to be active in the leadership process rather than defer to distinct differences between leaders and followers.

Consistent with the semi-structured interview findings, which posited the IFIVE board as very effective, their business plan (2006) data served to illustrate a primary value-added contribution, which is rendered by this board to their institution and region. That contribution can be aptly described as the collective or shared leadership enhancement of long-term quality, vitality, and stability of the institution. Several direct, positive, and futuristic statements within the business plan serve to illustrate this condition.

They are as follows:

1. The board approved plan clearly separates its goals from its strategic directions. The goal headings include – building communities through learning, targeted growth, and focus on learning for the future.

2. The plan articulates five strategic directions which are different from the goals and serve as roadmaps for reaching the goals. One example of the same – IFIVE will become a leader in the development of healthy and vibrant communities in our region.

3. Changes in the needs of employers in the region are emerging as the economy grows and changes. In addition, changes in the nature of health care services are resulting in the need to develop new approaches to the training of graduates.

4. There is an increasing expectation that colleges will be actively involved in increasing the participation rate of under-represented groups in postsecondary education. It was thought that this will mitigate the increasing shortage of skilled and unskilled labour in the province. Immigrant, aboriginal, and women in non-traditional employment sectors are examples of these under-represented groups. In addition, there are increasing expectations that higher level programming will be made available regionally. This will include better and more affordable access to degree and technology programs.

Lastly, as illustrated in Figure 2.0, unlike their counterpart college, ITWO, who used 2004-2005 data, the college utilized 2005-2006 projected revenues to support their 2006-2010 business plan.

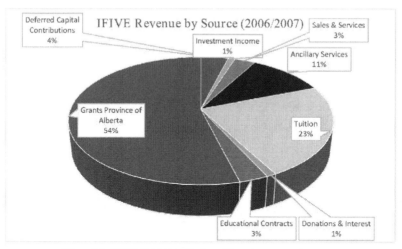

Figure 2.0 - IFIVE 2006-2010 Business Plan – i.e. revenue by source

Board Policies Analysis

Introduction

The second set of common documents chosen for analysis was the board policies of each of the two colleges. The board policies underwent a second coding and analysis according to source and type and were coded using a modified pattern of shared leadership categories, as developed by Chait, Ryan and Taylor (2005), which outline the three modes of governance as leadership – (1) fiduciary, (2) strategic, and (3) generative.

For the purposes of this analysis, the fiduciary mode of thinking and working together is characterized as the board's focus being with the stewardship of the tangible assets of the organization. The strategic mode is characterized by the board's focus on envisioning and shaping institutional direction. Lastly, the generative mode of thinking and working together is characterized by the board's focus on the provision of problems and opportunities towards a new field of knowledge complete with a new perspective (i.e. a paradigm shift).

TABLE 10
ITWO Board Policies (2007)

ITWO Board Policies		Mode of Governance Addressed		
Policy #	Policy Name	Fiduciary	Strategic	Generative
1	College Mission, Vision, Values and Mandate	X		X
2	Role of the Board	X	X	X
3	Role of Governor		X	X
4	Governor Code of Ethics	X	X	
5	Role of the Board Chair	X	X	X
6	Role of the Vice-Chair	X	X	
7	Board Operations	X	X	X
8	Committees of the Board	X	X	X
9	Board Representatives		X	X
10	Policy Making	X	X	X
11	Board Delegation of Authority	X	X	
12	Role of the President	X	X	X
13	Advocacy			X

As illustrated above in Table 10, the ITWO board appears to have fostered a balanced approach as to how they choose to think and work together. The board, which is characterized as a committee-rich environment, meets approximately five times a year as a group, and roughly five times in committee(s) on alternate months. An in-camera session is not specifically set out in policy or in agendas; however, it is identified as 'times when the public interest is best served by private discussion of specific issues.' A quorum is a simple majority.

TABLE 11
IFIVE Board Policies (2006)

IFIVE Board Policies		Mode of Governance Addressed		
Policy #	Policy Name	Fiduciary	Strategic	Generative
E1	Mission			X
E2	Workforce Knowledge and Skills Foundation			X
E3	Knowledge and Skills Foundation – For Further Post-Secondary Education			X
E4	Life Long Learning			X
E5	Enabling Community and Economic Development			X
GP-1	Global Governance Process	X		X
GP-2	Key Values Held	X	X	X
GP-3	Governing Style	X	X	X
GP-4	Board Job Description	X	X	X
GP-5	Chair's Role	X	X	X
GP-6	Board Committee Principles and Structure	X	X	X
GP-6.1	Audit Committee – Terms of Reference	X	X	
GP-7	Board Remuneration	X	X	X

IFIVE Board Policies - continued		Mode of Governance Addressed		
Policy #	Policy Name	Fiduciary	Strategic	Generative
GP-8	Code of Conduct	X	X	X
GP-9	Conflict of Interest	X		X
GP-10	Investment in Governance Process	X	X	X
GP-11	Board Linkage with Owners	X		
GP-12	Board Linkage with Other Organizations	X		X
GP-13	Board Planning Cycle and Agenda	X	X	X
GP-14	Board Member Selection Process		X	X
GP-15	Recruitment Process		X	X
GP-16	Board Retreat Purpose and Scope	X	X	
EL-A1	Treatment of Staff			X
EL-A2	Compensation and Benefits	X		X
EL-A3	Executive Succession		X	X
EL-A4	Participation and Treatment of Learners		X	X
EL-B1	General Executive Constraint			X
EL-B2	Communication and Support to the Board		X	
EL-B3	Public Image		X	X
EL-C1	Financial Planning	X		
EL-C2	Financial Condition	X	X	
EL-C3	Asset Protection	X	X	
EL-C4	Tuition Fees	X		
EL-D1	Curriculum and Instruction	X		X
EL-D2	Program Changes	X	X	
EL-D3	Ethical Research	X		
EL-D4	Entrepreneurial Activity and Partnerships	X	X	X

IFIVE Board Policies - continued		Mode of Governance Addressed		
Policy #	Policy Name	Fiduciary	Strategic	Generative
BC-1	Delegation to the President	X	X	
BC-2	President Job Description	X	X	
BC-3	Monitoring Executive Performance	X	X	X
BC-4	Employer/Employee Matters		X	

As illustrated in Table 11, the IFIVE board appears to have fostered a balanced approach as to how they have chosen to think and work together. The most significant difference in the governance approach of the IFIVE board from their counterpart, the ITWO board, seems to be in the overall size of the body of work encompassed within their sphere of influence. For example, as illustrated in Table 10, the ITWO board body of work, which is generative in nature, is supported by 10 broad based policy development areas. In the case of the IFIVE board, the body of work, which is generative in nature, as well, is supported by 28 broad based policy development areas.

The IFIVE board policies are divided into four classic areas. They are as follows: (1) ends [E], (2) governance process [GP], (3) executive limitations [EL], and (4) board-president relationships [BC]. Within their board planning cycle and agenda control policy, outlined in Policy #GP-13, it stated that the board will meet 10 times per calendar year. These meetings are sub-divided as follows: (1) three learning workshop sessions, and (2) seven public board meetings with seven in-camera meetings. Consistent with the semi-structured interview input, by both the board chair and the president, the board has a very high value for board education and training and as illustrated in Policy #GP-16.

According to the ITWO board chair and as identified in the semi-structured interviews analysis, the ITWO board is said to understand shared leadership and have demonstrated the same by their focus on policy development and institutional performance. The data presented in Table 10 tended to refute this claim on the basis of a small body of primary work (policy development) along with stale-dated policies, which have not been reviewed on an annual basis. In contrast, according to the IFIVE president, as identified in the semi-structured interviews analysis, the IFIVE board is said to have exhibited a good understanding of shared leadership and have demonstrated the same by their focus on policy development and institutional performance. The data presented in Table 11 tended to substantiate this claim on the basis of a significantly large body of primary work (policy development), supported by an annual policy review process, and regularly policy-related discussion items on each board meeting agenda.

Performance Envelope Measures Analysis

Introduction

The third set of common documents and artifacts chosen for analysis was the Ministry of Advanced Education [and Technology] performance measures. This institution performance instrumentation, developed by the Ministry of Advanced Education (2006), annually identifies five key performance indicators, which are tracked and aggregated into a performance envelope scorecard. It in turn, is used to provide an incentive for certain behaviors and to award incremental revenues to higher performing institutions. Each indicator has an assigned point value. For example, employment rate of graduates, graduate satisfaction, and accessibility are assigned 30 points each, whereas administrative expenses, as a function of overall expenses, and enterprise revenue generation are assigned five points each. Hence, upon submission of the key performance indicator data, by the respective institution, the Ministry is able to calculate the performance envelope totals for each institution, out of a possible score of 100, and provide corresponding financial awards for higher performing institutions.

ITWO Performance Envelope Results		
	Total Points (out of 100)	System Average
Year 1: 2004-2005	94.0	85.9
Year 2: 2005-2006	93.0	81.6
Year 3: 2006-2007	84.0	79.5
3 Year Average	90.3	82.3

IFIVE Performance Envelope Results		
	Total Points (out of 100)	System Average
Year 1: 2004-2005	97.0	85.9
Year 2: 2005-2006	87.0	81.6
Year 3: 2006-2007	87.0	79.5
3 Year Average	90.3	82.3

TABLE 12
Summary of All Performance Envelope Data for the Past Three Years

Year 1: 2004-2005

Institution	Employment Rate		Graduate Satisfaction		Accessibility		Administrative Expenses		Enterprise Revenue		Total Points
	Points	Benchmarks	Points	Benchmarks	Points	Benchmarks	Points	Benchmarks	Points	Benchmarks	
IONE	30	93.2	30	96.9	20	-0.26	3	8.7	3	23.9	86.0
ITWO	30	94.8	30	97.2	30	11.05	0	13.0	4	25.2	94.0
ITHREE	30	94.2	25	89.8	30	4.45	4	8.0	4	25.4	93.0
IFOUR	30	96.2	30	95.2	20	-2.81	3	8.9	3	22.7	86.0
IFIVE	30	91.5	30	96.7	30	3.98	3	7.7	4	29.4	97.0
ISIX	30	96.5	30	95.1	30	7.88	0	12.1	1	8.1	91.0
ISEVEN	30	96.3	20	85.5	0	-22.63	1	13.4	3	10.0	53.0
IEIGHT	30	96.4	30	95.4	20	-2.08	3	9.7	4	25.9	87.0
System Wide	30.0	94.9	28.1	94.0	22.5	-0.1	2.0	10.2	3.3	21.3	85.9

Year 2: 2005-2006

Institution	Employment Rate		Graduate Satisfaction		Accessibility		Administrative Expenses		Enterprise Revenue		Total Points
	Points	Benchmarks	Points	Benchmarks	Points	Benchmarks	Points	Benchmarks	Points	Benchmarks	
IONE	30	93.2	30	96.9	25	3.17	3	8.5	3	21.5	91.0
ITWO	30	94.8	30	97.2	30	8.10	0	13.1	3	23.6	93.0
ITHREE	30	94.2	25	89.8	25	3.43	4	7.4	4	26.8	88.0
IFOUR	30	96.2	30	95.2	20	-3.04	3	10.1	4	25.3	87.0
IFIVE	30	90.0	30	96.7	20	-0.86	3	8.0	4	28.4	87.0
ISIX	30	98.9	30	94.2	25	1.90	3	11.6	1	7.4	89.0
ISEVEN	30	96.3	20	85.5	0	-27.72	0	12.7	1	7.5	51.0
IEIGHT	30	96.4	30	95.4	20	-7.33	3	11.3	4	26.7	67.0
System Wide	30.0	95.0	28.1	93.9	18.1	-2.8	2.4	10.3	3.0	20.9	81.6

Institution	Employment Rate		Graduate Satisfaction		Accessibility		Administrative Expenses		Enterprise Revenue		Total Points
	Points	Benchmarks	Points	Benchmarks	Points	Benchmarks	Points	Benchmarks	Points	Benchmarks	
IONE	30	95.4	30	89.9	20	-0.7	3	8.9	3	19.8	86.0
ITWO	30	97.4	30	91.6	20	-3.0	0	12.7	4	28.8	84.0
ITHREE	30	96.1	25	87.6	20	-0.7	4	7.4	4	25.7	83.0
IFOUR	30	95.9	30	93.0	20	-4.5	0	11.6	4	25.4	84.0
IFIVE	30	97.5	30	94.7	20	-1.2	3	8.4	4	24.6	87.0
ISIX	30	98.9	30	94.2	25	1.9	3	11.6	1	7.4	89.0
ISEVEN	25	82.1	30	90.7	0	-15.4	3	12.0	1	8.8	59.0
IEIGHT	30	97.1	30	91.8	0	-8.7	0	14.0	4	28.1	64.0
System Wide	30.0	95.1	29.4	91.7	15.6	-4.0	2.0	10.8	3.1	21.1	79.5

Comments

From a review of the summary of performance envelope data, as illustrated above in Table 12, it would appear that both institutions have performed significantly above the system average. ITWO recorded a three-year average score of 90.3 compared to a system average of 82.3. Likewise IFIVE recorded a three-year average score of 90.3.

Over the past three years, both institutions scored within four points of one another in the employment rate of graduates and graduate satisfaction key performance indicators. Somewhat similarly, both institutions have begun to be impacted by declining enrolment. In the case of ITWO, their enrolment decline over the past two years has begun to affect their scorecard and will continue to do so over the next few years as the calculation is based upon a three-year rolling average. As evidenced in their business plan, ITWO is further impacted in this regard as they have initiated a reduction of certificate based programs, which have proven to be unsustainable. With reference to

IFIVE declining enrolment challenges, their business plan cited causal factors such as the robust nature of the Alberta economy and the constant urbanization effect on rural communities.

Outside of equivalent results over the past three years by both institutions relative to the enterprise revenue generation indicator, the only other major difference in their results can be found in the analysis of their administrative expenses as a percentage of their overall institutional expenses. Consistent with their business plan comments, which reflected a high cost structure on the administrative side of the operations, with campuses in three large communities, ITWO has been challenged significantly in this regard over the past three years and has not accrued any points towards their overall scorecard.

Lastly, and consistent with the ITWO semi-structured interview responses and analysis, which reflected a less effective board environment, it appeared to be compounded by an autocratic leadership factor. As well, without a collective value for shared leadership, a key concern with their three-year results would be the overall downward trend of their accessibility indicator and the institution's overall performance envelope totals.

Survey Questionnaire

Background

The survey questionnaire was sequenced to follow the semi-structured interviews and document collection. It was administered electronically in May

2007, to all board members serving the eight non-metro colleges. By Alberta government legislation the composition of each public college board is composed as follows: (1) board chairperson, (2) six other publicly appointed members, (3) the president, (4) one faculty representative, (5) one staff representative, and (6) one student representative.

The results of the survey questionnaire were intended to provide a comparative representation of the institutions. As well, they were intended to provide quantitative measures against which the qualitative assessments of the semi-structured interviews could be compared within the institution(s) and the non-metro system at large. The seven-page survey questionnaire was subjected to a two-stage testing process and included closed questions, an introduction, respondent background information, and one substantive question.

Response Rate

The survey questionnaire was e-mailed to 88 board members representing eight non-metro Western Canadian public colleges. Potential respondents were informed in the introduction that participation in the study was voluntary and that individual responses would be confidential. It would appear that the response rate was influenced by the fact that many of the eight student representatives to their respective boards had completed their one-year board appointments by May, and thus, did not respond. As well, the rate may have been influenced by several of the eight board chairs and eight presidents who chose not to complete the questionnaire because they felt that they had responded in person through the semi-structured interview process. Additionally, the rate may have been influenced by a small percentage of relatively new board members who chose not to complete the questionnaire due to their perceived lack of sufficient knowledge and experience as a governor.

Data Coding

Data collected from the survey questionnaires were numerically coded as follows:

Age	Chronological age in years.
Gender Ratio	Male and female ratio(s) based upon the number of individuals
Educational Level	Less than high school (1), high school (2), college (3), university/professional (4), and graduate degree (5)
Shared Leadership Understanding (SLU)	Questions 1a to 1h. A response of yes = 1 and no = 0.
Shared Leadership Practicing (SLP)	Questions 2a to 2h. A response of yes = 1 and no = 0.
Focus on Institutional Performance (FIP)	Questions 3a to 3e. The coding was based upon the system-wide average of 10 board meetings per annum. Therefore, every board meeting = 10, once every 3-4 months = 4, once a year = 1, and never = 0.

President's Governance-related Knowledge, Skills, and Abilities Associated with the Board's Practice of Shared Leadership and Board Governance (PG-KSA)	Questions 4a, 4b, and 4d. The coding was based upon every board meeting = 10, once every 3-4 months = 4, once a year = 1, and never = 0.
Board's Competencies which Underscore Board Governance Efficiency (BC)	Questions 5a to 5f. A response of yes = 1 and no = 0.
Board's Human Capital Mix (HC Mix)	Questions 6a to 6e. A response of yes = 1 and no = 0.

Data Presentation and Summary

Table 13 reflects the aforementioned numerical coding system and the Pearson Product Moment correlation values using CoStat version 6.311. As mentioned, institutional mean values for the parameters were used to derive the Pearson Product Moment correlation coefficient values, which measure the linear association of two independent variables.

Strong Correlations

A strong correlation between two factors indicated that factors strongly influence one another. SLU correlated strongly with SLP, PG-KSA, BC, HC Mix and KPIs; SLP also showed strong correlation to BC in addition to SLU. A strong correlation existed between BC and, SLU, SLP, HC Mix and KPIs. FIP correlated strongly only with HC Mix.

TABLE 13.   Correlation Matrix from Data from the Survey Questionnaire

	Age	Gender Ratio	Educ.	SLU	SLP	FIP	PG-KSA	BC	HC Mix	KPI 04/05	KPI 05/06	KPI 05/06	KPI AVG
Age	-												
Gender Ratio (M/F)	0.8427	-											
Education	0.3441	0.6201	-										
Shared Leadership Understanding (SLU)	-0.0753	-0.1126	0.2967	-									
Shared Leadership Practice (SLP)	0.0599	-0.0703	0.0874	0.3413	-								
Focus on Institutional Performance (FIP)	-0.1672	0.0126	0.6771	0.5322	0.2390	-							
President's Governance Knowledge, Skills and Ability (PG-KSA)	0.4327	0.2423	0.6075	0.7650	0.6926	0.6307	-						
Boards Competency (BC)	-0.0701	0.2371	0.2972	0.9461	0.8840	0.3862	0.5287	-					
Human Capital Mix (HC Mix)	-0.4170	0.0562	0.3754	0.7488	0.5608	0.7382	0.5000	0.7955	-				
Performance 2004-2005 (KPI 04/05)	-0.0625	0.0918	0.4545	0.6504	0.5659	0.4029	0.4448	0.3224	0.6994	-			
Performance 2005-2006 (KPI 05/06)	0.0396	0.2307	0.2323	0.7672	0.6712	0.5135	0.6809	0.7525	0.6296	0.6586	-		
Performance 2006-2007 (KPI 06/07)	0.0831	0.1069	0.4281	0.8291	0.7924	0.4635	0.7785	0.7485	0.6516	0.7720	0.8659	-	
3 Year KPI Average (KPI Avg.)	0.0173	0.1513	0.3878	0.7761	0.7015	0.4892	0.6565	0.8763	0.6917	0.9252	0.9341	0.9466	-

* Shaded cells indicate strong correlation between parameter at 95% Confidence limit (p<0.05)

*Shaded cells indicate strong correlation between parameter at 95%
Confidence limit (p<0.05)

160

Demographics Discussion

From a system wide perspective, the average age of the respondent was 52.3 years, predominately their education level was some level of higher education, and the gender distribution was skewed towards the male population. The response rate per institution ranged from a high of 81.8% to a low of 27.3%. There were a total of six boards with response rates of 45% or higher.

Discussion of Key Concepts and Factors

Understanding of Shared Leadership

The survey questionnaire results, as shown in Table 13, demonstrated a very strong correlation of 0.9413 existed between a board's understanding of shared leadership and their practicing of shared leadership. Similarly, the results demonstrated a very strong correlation of 0.8481 between a board's understanding of shared leadership and the board's competency level.

As well, the results indicated a very strong correlation of 0.7552 existed between a board's understanding of shared leadership and the president's governance knowledge, skills, and abilities. Likewise, a very strong correlation of 0.7468 was found to exist between a board's understanding of shared leadership and the human capital mix of the board. Lastly, the matrix indicated very strong correlations existed between a board's understanding of shared leadership and institutional performance, particularly in the years of 2005-2006 (0.7572), 2006-2007 (0.8291), and in the overall three-year key performance indicator average at 0.7764.

161

The results indicated that an understanding of shared leadership should be a board's primary concern in relation to their practice of shared leadership and the building of board competency. Also, they suggest that a board, who wishes to influence institutional performance, be diligent in the development of their board member recruitment policies and practices, specifically in two domains. Firstly, as an outcome of their hiring and succession policies and practices, they should ensure a president is hired and developed with governance knowledge, skills, and abilities. Secondly, within their board member recruitment policies and practices, they should ensure an ongoing and rich human capital mix within their board membership.

As indicated in Table 14, all colleges SLU questionnaire results would appear to be consistent with the analysis of the comments within the semi-structured interviews. These results are evidenced by the four institutions with boards, which practice shared leadership, and were previously designated to be highly effective boards (i.e. institutions IONE, ITHREE, IFIVE, and ISIX).

TABLE 14
Shared Leadership Understanding (SLU) – All Colleges

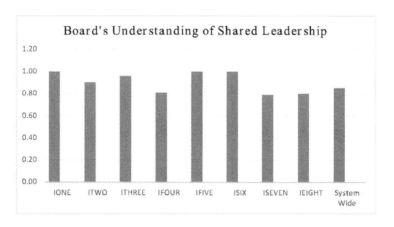

Note: The Positive Response Index (PRI) on Y axis represented the institutional mean value. In all cases PRI values are between 0 and 1. The magnitude of the PRI for an institution denoted the level of an affirmative response to the statement or question by all respondents from the institution. For example, when the PRI for an institution is 0.8, on the average, 80% of respondents from the institution agreed with the question or statement.

Practicing of Shared Leadership

The survey questionnaire results, as demonstrated in Table 13, indicated that a board's practicing of shared leadership correlated very strongly at 0.8047 with the competency of the board. As well, the results showed a very strong correlation level of 0.7924 for the board's practicing of shared leadership within the 2006-2007 performance of the institution. The results

163

appear to underscore the importance of understanding and practicing shared leadership as foundational underpinnings to the building of board competency and impacting institutional performance.

As indicated in Table 15, all colleges SLP questionnaire results would appear to be consistent with the analysis of the comments within the semi-structured interviews. These results are evidenced by the four institutions with boards, which practiced shared leadership on a regular basis, and were previously designated to be highly effective boards (i.e. institutions IONE, ITHREE, IFIVE, and ISIX).

TABLE 15
Shared Leadership Practicing (SLP) – All Colleges

Focus on Institutional Performance

As indicated in Table 13, a focus on institutional performance appeared to have a very strong correlation of 0.7562 with the human capital mix of the board's membership. One interpretation of this result might suggest a need for a diversity theme to underscore board member recruitment policies and practices. The results may suggest that it is not advisable for a board to accumulate too much of a certain type of human capital should a focus on institutional performance be desired. Rather, these results might indicate the need for a more diverse approach to the human capital mix within the board's membership, which may include such forms as intellectual, reputational, political, and social capital.

As indicated in Table 16, all colleges FIP questionnaire would appear to be consistent with analysis of the comments within the semi-structured interviews. These results particularly apply to the boards of institutions ITHREE and ISIX, who practice shared leadership, and were previously designated as highly effective. Upon review of the semi-structured interview results, it was noted that these two boards and their officials reflected high to very high contribution levels regarding the extent of contribution of the board's human capital mix. In contrast, the official(s) of institution IONE, with a board deemed to be highly effective, demonstrated some discrepancy in their responses to the extent of contribution of the board's human capital mix factor.

TABLE 16
Focus on Institutional Performance (FIP) – All Colleges

The survey questionnaire results raised a couple of interesting questions. Could a highly effective board such as IFIVE, as noted in Table 17, understand and practice shared leadership; however, not choose to focus on the institution's performance as defined by the government's key performance indicators? Furthermore, is it possible that the same board – sharing high and very high reflective values for factors like the president's governance knowledge, skills, and abilities, and the board's human capital mix - may focus only on what they define to be the institution's key performance indicators?

TABLE 17
Focus on Institutional Performance – IFIVE Board

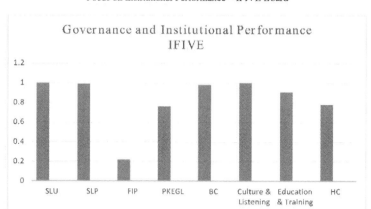

Governance and Institutional Performance
IFIVE

President's Competency and Performance

The survey questionnaire results indicated a very strong correlation of 0.7769 existed between the president's governance knowledge, skills, and abilities and the 2006-2007 performance of the institution. As evidenced earlier, with a strong correlation of 0.7552, the results support the relationship of the president's governance knowledge, skills, and abilities to a board's understanding and practicing of shared leadership, and ultimately to the institution's performance. In interpreting this set of relationships, one could posit that it is incumbent on a board, who wishes to impact institutional performance, to be diligent in their search for a new president and/or in the professional development of the one they have chosen.

As indicated in Table 18, all colleges' KG-KSA questionnaire results would appear to be consistent with the analysis of the comments within the semi-structured interviews. These results are evidenced by three of the four institutions with boards, who practice shared leadership and were previously designated as very effective (i.e. institutions IONE, IFIVE, and ISIX).

There is however, one notable anomaly – the ITWO board. This board, which was previously designated as less effective, demonstrated a strong correlation between the president's governance knowledge, skills, and abilities, and the board's practicing of shared leadership. Two possible explanations may explain this result. One, the ITWO board accepted the resignation of their president a little over a year ago. Two, the unproven president of ITWO, had been on the job for less than nine months at the time of the administration of the survey questionnaire.

TABLE 18
President's Governance Knowledge, Skills, and Abilities (PG-KSA)

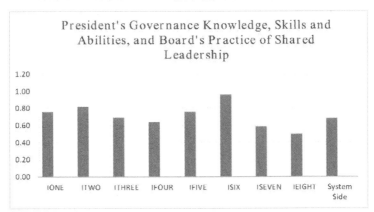

Governance-Related Education and Training

The survey questionnaire results, as illustrated in Table 13, exhibited a very strong correlation of 0.7468 existing between the board's human capital mix and their shared leadership understanding. Additionally, a very strong correlation of 0.7905 was evidenced between the human capital mix and the competency of the board. It should be noted that the competency of the board(s) was tested in the survey questionnaire by utilizing the six skill sets, as outlined in *The Effective Board of Trustees* (Chait, Holland, and Taylor 1995).

One interpretation of the board competency data may be centered in the governance-related education and training of board members, who appear to come from diverse backgrounds and experiences. Because of the complex nature of today's higher education and community-related issues, which may impact non-metro colleges, there appears to be a growing need for boards to possess governance knowledge at a relatively high level. Some examples of this knowledge capacity, which should influence the growth of board competency, include the following: (1) policy governance, (2) strategic and generative thinking, (3) community development, (4) business and industry knowledge, (5) risk management, (6) technology, and (7) financial management. Hence, given the very strong correlation which existed between the human capital mix of a board and their competency level, it appears reasonable to assume that there is a need for governance-related education and training to improve their governance knowledge levels.

Questions 5b and 5c of the questionnaire sought responses from all board members regarding their ideas relative to education and training of individual members and the professional development of the board as a working group. In relation to board governance efficiency these education and training question results are presented in Table 19. It is noteworthy to mention that the all college education and training questionnaire results would appear to be consistent, as well, with the analysis of the comments within the semi-structured interviews. These results are evidenced by the four institutions with boards, which practice shared leadership and were previously designated to be very effective (i.e. institutions IONE, ITHREE, IFIVE, and ISIX).

TABLE 19
Governance-Related Education and Training – All Colleges

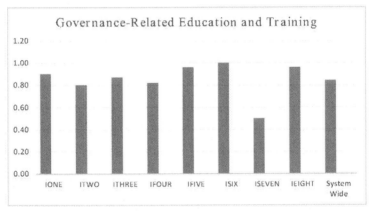

Human Capital Composition or Mix

Another interpretation of the data, as demonstrated in Table 20, may be the presence of good appointment processes that result in the selection of

170

effective board members and chairpersons. Processes in institutions that practice shared leadership appear to be more proactive and based in policy. These processes have the tendency to enhance the pool of qualified applicants and build public confidence in the recruitment of board members.

Additionally, as indicated in Table 20, all colleges HC Mix questionnaire results would appear to be consistent with the analysis of the comments within the semi-structured interviews. These results are evidenced by three of the four institutions with boards, who practice shared leadership and were previously designated to be very effective (i.e. institutions ITHREE, IFIVE, and ISIX).

TABLE 20
Human Capital Mix (HC) – All Colleges

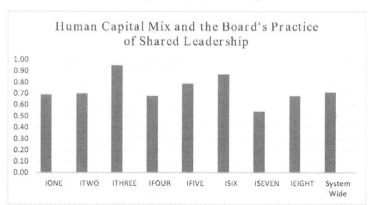

One additional comment is offered regarding the notable exception from the group of very effective boards as seen in Table 20 – i.e. the human capital mix results of the IONE board. It is interesting to note that during the semi-structured interviews the president of IONE, a board member, assigned a low contribution level to this factor. Given that the president, with considerable experience, has the capacity to be instrumental in the recruitment and appointment of new board members, the matrix results may be more reflective of individual values than a function of shared leadership practicing.

Stewardship and Listeners to the College's Voice

The survey questionnaire results, as shown in Table 13, demonstrate that board competency correlated very strongly at 0.8481 with the understanding of shared leadership and at 0.8047 with the practice of shared leadership. In interpreting these results, from a competency building perspective, one could purport the board's need for well-defined roles and responsibilities in the understanding and practicing of shared leadership. As well, accepting that competency capacity-building is a function of a clear purpose, one may posit that a board should place an emphasis early in their tenure, on the facilitation of the institution's values, vision, mission, and outcomes. In addition, the board competency correlated very strongly at 0.7905 with the human capital mix factor. As well, board competency correlated very strongly with the key performance indicator data associated with institutional performance in all three years – 2004-2005 (0.8224), 2005-2006 (0.7825), and 2006-2007 (0.7487), as well as the three year key performance indicator average at 0.8062. Clearly, no other governance-related factor appears to have the same level of influence on institutional performance.

It should be noted that the matrix reflected board competency data, collected from board members that measured six dimensions of an effective governing board, as proposed by Chait, Holland, and Taylor (1996). The dimensions were as follows: (1) contextual, (2) educational, (3) interpersonal, (4) analytical, (5) political, and (6) strategic. With respect to the contextual, interpersonal, and political dimensions two questions within the survey questionnaire – 5a and 5e – probed the member's sentiments relative to their regard for institutional culture and norms, listening to the college's voice, as well as their need to develop healthy relationships among major stakeholders. The results of these stewardship-related questions are illustrated below in Table 21.

TABLE 21
The Board's Stewardship Competencies – All Colleges

As illustrated in Table 21, with the exception of IEIGHT, all institutions appeared to universally endorse the need for board to see themselves as being sensitive to the institution's culture and norms, listeners to the college's voice and mindful of their stakeholder advocacy responsibilities. Of note, is the fact that no other governance-related factor received such wide-spread endorsement in the data. The unusually low score exhibited by IEIGHT may be explainable, given the degree of healing the board has undergone over the past nine months following the termination of their president at the beginning of the 2006-2007 academic session. As Carver (1997) stated, "the CEO's only job is to make everything come out right! That translates into achieving the board's ends policies and not violating its executive limitations policies (p. 113). As was outlined during the semi-structured interviews with the IEIGHT board chair, the board shared part of the blame in the termination as they may have been less than diligent in their accountability, planning, and reporting procedures, specifically as they applied to the ongoing monitoring of ends policies and executive limitations.

Board Competency

Lastly, as shown in Table 22, all colleges BC questionnaire results would appear to be consistent with the analysis of the comments within the semi-structured interviews. These results are evidenced by the four institutions with boards, which practice shared leadership and were previously designated to be very effective (i.e. institutions IONE, ITHREE, IFIVE, and ISIX).

TABLE 22
Board Competency – All Colleges

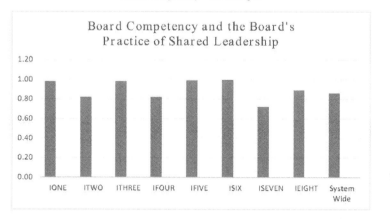

Board Competency and the Board's Practice of Shared Leadership

After coding and quantitative analysis of all survey questionnaire responses to question seven, no correlation was found between responses (Y or N) to questions at a 95% confidence limit, nor to any of the factors as demonstrated in Table 21. However, after coding of the responses, which were grouped based upon institution, the qualitative analysis of question seven tends to support the findings of the semi-structured interviews, and specifically, the analysis of the documents and artifacts as they applied to the boards of ITWO (less effective) and IFIVE (very effective).

Major Research Questions Discussion

Question One

> To what extent do board members in Western Canadian rural, public colleges understand the eight concepts of shared leadership (SLU) and board governance effectiveness?

All respondents (100%) during the semi-structured interviews exhibited a good understanding of the shared leadership concepts and indicated that their board members shared a good understanding, as well. Apparently, as evidenced in the data of at least two of the eight boards, a good understanding of the concepts does not appear to be sufficient to guarantee the practicing of shared leadership nor exceptional effectiveness.

For instance, as profiled in the document and artifact analysis, one of the two boards (ITWO), which was seen as less effective, focused primarily on their fiduciary role ensuring integrity and compliance with the law. Strategic planning, as outlined in the board approved business plan, was essentially a function of chairperson and president discussions, and policy development, which could reflect their understanding of shared leadership. In contrast, within the same analysis, one of the boards, IFIVE, which was seen as very effective, appeared to add active engagement and independent decision making to their underlying fiduciary, strategic, and generative debates. Their documentation seemed to reflect collegiality and openness with one another and their president.

Bolman and Deal (1997) submitted that a caring community requires servant-leaders who serve the best interests of the community and its stakeholders. This [state] implies a profound and challenging responsibility for leaders to understand the needs and concerns of members in order to serve the best interests of individuals and the community as a whole (pp. 346-347). Strong boards and strong presidents, who understand the shared leadership concepts, make for good governance providing that they put this understanding into practice. The foregoing data would tend to support the idea that in an integrated community setting, an understanding of shared leadership may be the foundational factor associated with the provision of servant leadership, board effectiveness, and organizational performance. Sharing a passion for serving their communities and publics, the board and the president tend to forge a dynamic relationship that can lead to a higher level of performance.

Question Two

> *To what extent do boards of rural, public colleges practice the*
> *six characteristics of shared leadership (SLP)?*

Outside of one institution's board, ITWO, the results suggested that all seven boards tended to practice the six characteristics of shared leadership to varying degrees at one time or another throughout the academic year. In the case of the ITWO board, although the chairperson stated a desire to have his board informed, engaged, and responsible – in practice, the president appeared to be disconnected from board members, who appeared to perform their role(s) in a limited communication environment.

In contrast, the document and artifact analysis of a very effective board yielded a different set of results, which demonstrated a practice of the six characteristics of shared leadership. A review of the business plan and policy handbook of the IFIVE board indicated a delegation of operations to their president, while reserving to themselves, organizational oversight and policy setting. Clearly, the analysis of the data reflected a large body of strategic and generative work by the board, which provided support and direction to their president and the institution. The evidence suggested that the board recognized that they cannot govern well without the president's collaboration and that the president cannot lead the organization consistently with the ends without the board's support and direction.

Lastly, the documentation characterized the board's partnership with the president with mutual trust, forthrightness, and a common commitment to the college's values. Likewise, the data suggested that very effective boards tend to govern in constructive partnership with their president and his or her senior administrative team, recognizing that the effectiveness of the board and the president are interdependent.

Question Three

> *To what extent does the institution's performance (FIP) reflect*
> *the degree of shared leadership practiced by the board of a rural,*
> *public college?*

The results demonstrated that 75% of the respondents agreed at the high or very high reflection level with the idea that the institution's performance reflected the board's practice of shared leadership. In focusing on institutional performance, very effective boards, which practice shared leadership, tend to allocate the majority of their time to substantive issues, moving away from report-driven formats and towards agendas that provoke meaningful discussion and debate that shape institutional strategy and actions. In collaboration with their president, they appear to help clarify problems, offer externally-based insights on issues, and offer alternatives for framing opportunities and challenges.

Upon analysis of the documents and artifacts, the IFIVE board, which was seen as very effective, focused on institutional performance by clearly articulating its strategic directions and goals. In doing so, the goals are separated from the strategic directions and identify macro institutional initiatives such as the building of communities through learning and focus on learning for the future. Whereas, the ITWO board, which was seen as less effective, presented goals in their planning and policy documents that appeared more like values – i.e. quality, access, affordability, diversity, and collaboration. The IFIVE board, when presenting their strategic directions appeared to be providing "roadmaps" for reaching their stated goals. For example, they aspire to become a leader in the development of healthy and vibrant communities in their region of the Province. In contrast, the ITWO board, related institutional performance to the government's commitment to operational funding. For example, they indicated that rural colleges, such as themselves, looked forward to continued envelopes of provincial funding as the primary source of expanding their core programming. Furthermore, the analysis provided insight into the ITWO board's unmonitored focus on institutional performance being directly related to an obsession with cost pressures and their control.

In summary, the data supports the idea that very effective boards appear to allocate time and focus to what matters most and continuously engage in strategic and generative thinking to shape the institution's direction. They appear to translate strategic priorities into action plans, in concert with their president, identifying ways that they may contribute to the institution's success. Their business plans, policy statements, and agendas seem to reflect their strategic directions as a basis for institutional and presidential assessment and the fine-tuning of future plans.

Question Four

> *What is the extent of the contribution of each of the governance factors towards board effectiveness?*

President's (Governance) Competency and Performance (PG-KSA) Factor

The semi-structured interviews analysis of the data noted that 87.5% of all board chairperson comments reflected their concurrence at the high to very high contribution level relative to the extent of contribution made by the president's [governance] competency and performance towards board effectiveness. Additionally, 62.5% of all president comments reflected their concurrence at the high to very high contribution level. Generally, the data supported the idea that the board and the president bring important and complementary elements to the shared leadership concept that, when aggregated, were seen to be greater than the sum of their parts. The results suggest that very effective boards have strong, talented, and honest presidents who provided their respective boards with the tools and information to govern very effectively.

When considering the document and artifact data, in relation to the importance of the president's [governance] competency, one can clearly see the chief executive's influence, or lack thereof, in the linkages between the governance ends and the academic plan of the college. A very effective board, such as IFIVE, with a strong president holds their chief executive accountable annually and formally. They continuously assess the institution's performance in relation to presidential performance. A less effective board, like ITWO, with an unproven president, shows little evidence of encouraging their chief executive to strengthen necessary skills, or providing the chief executive with the opportunity to influence policy development in the form of values, vision, mission and outcomes.

In conclusion, if we assume that a president's performance appraisal is the primary measure boards utilize for assessing institutional performance; given the results of the survey questionnaire and the other data; would it not be advisable for boards to align with ministry vision, outcomes and key performance indicators in assessing their president quantitatively and on the basis of the institution's performance? This study found little to no evidence in any of the eight institutions of such a practice or set of policies.

All of this may suggest that much work lies ahead in terms of the alignment of ministry goals and those of the institution(s). The government of

Alberta has the primary legal responsibility for the governance of their public institutions – the exercise and assignment of authority and power – which appears to call into question the parameters of their ongoing governance responsibility to support the institution and its president.

Board's Human Capital Composition or Mix (HC Mix) Factor with a discussion regarding the Governance-related Education and Training Factor

The analysis of the results indicated that 100% of all board chairperson comments reflected their concurrence at the high to very high contribution level with the extent of the contribution made by the board's human capital mix towards board effectiveness. As well, 62.5% of all president comments reflected their concurrence at the high to very high contribution level with this factor. Very effective boards tend to embrace diversity of membership and recognize that effectiveness depends upon attention to group dynamics. They readily see the correlation between institutional performance, strategic planning, and board mix. They seek diversity and inclusiveness. In concert with their presidents, very effective boards appeared to create an environment based upon respect and candor, which provided a productive exchange of ideas. Questioning of one another is promoted, as well as challenges to the president and senior administration. Board members tend to aggregate and synthesize diverse viewpoints to advance the dialogue.

The semi-structured interviews analysis of the results elicited 50% of all board chairperson comments reflecting their concurrence at the high to very high contribution level with the extent of the contribution made by governance-related education and training to board effectiveness. As well,

50% of all president comments reflected their concurrence at the high to very high contribution level with this factor. Understanding that governance work does not always come naturally to boards, very effective boards appear to seek guidance in governance roles and responsibilities. They tend to ensure that all board members participate at a minimum in a formal orientation and some form of continuous education and training.

The analysis of the documentation and artifacts, relative to the human capital mix and governance-related education and training demonstrated a clear distinction between a very effective board and a less effective board in relation to policy development. Whereas a very effective board's policy development (IFIVE) reflected close attention to the composition and maximization of the board, a less effective board's policy development (ITWO) demonstrated a minimal amount of attention to this factor. For example, with reference to the IFIVE board policy development, articles were present in their policy handbook such as board member selection process, recruitment process, and board retreat purpose and scope. In stark contrast, the ITWO board policy handbook is practically devoid of any reference to board member recruitment, selection, or orientation.

In conclusion, Chait, Ryan and Taylor (2005) stated, "if boards launched campaigns to cultivate and deploy the members' intellectual, reputational, political, and social capital that were roughly comparable to efforts to garner the board members' financial resources, the results could yield substantial dividends" (p. 161). The professional expertise and personal experience that board members bring to the table is important; however, it does not seem to be sufficient for board effectiveness. The data suggested that through ongoing and targeted education and training, very effective boards appear to deepen members' knowledge about higher education, trends, and their institution's role in the bigger scheme of things. Additionally, very effective boards tend to recognize and understand the importance of fresh perspectives and the risks associated with cliques. They appear to assess continuous quality improvement and participation prior to extending terms and will remove less effective members to maintain a sense of shared responsibility among the board and with the administration.

Board Competency (BC) with a discussion regarding the Stewardship and Listeners to the College's Voice Factor

The semi-structured interviews analysis yielded 62.5% of all chairperson comments reflected their concurrence at the high to very high contribution level regarding the extent of the contribution made by the stewardship and listeners to the college's voice factor. As well, 75% of all president comments reflected their concurrence at the high to very high contribution level regarding this factor. Very effective boards appear to understand that it is in the institution's best interests to develop and maintain open, two-way relationships with staff, as well as external stakeholders and the larger community. Working with faculty, staff, students, and alumni, very effective boards tend to ensure that everyone is treated with respect and receives forthright reports on the board's happenings and developments. They seem to foster open exchanges between the board and staff members and readily receive information of significance from their various internal publics and put it to use in their strategic and generative planning.

The policy structure of a very effective board (IFIVE) ensures that staff feel comfortable bringing appropriate matters to their attention. Policy statements reflect how transparency informs board activities and planning and to what extent governance practices are made public. The document and artifact analysis provided an insight into the policy development and procedures associated with the promotion of a culture of transparency. Very effective boards appear to promote a culture of transparency by ensuring that interested members of the college community and the public have access to appropriate and accurate information regarding operations, finances, and results. In return, very effective boards' policy development reflected their desire to earn the public trust evidenced by whistle-blower policies, which protect the integrity of the institution and its staff.

Lastly, regardless of their composition or their level of governance development, the data implied that if competency capacity-building is the goal, boards should possess some basic competency sets such as: (1) willingness to ask good questions, (2) critical thinking with independent judgment, (3) commitment to the long-term interests, (4) be a good person with passion, dignity, and an ethical character, and (5) be focused, faithful, and disciplined.

Question Five

> *To what extent does the rural community's commitment and capacity to learn reflect its college board's proficiency to work in all three governance as leadership modes?*

The results of the semi-structured interviews appeared to be consistent across the spectrum of institutions with all claiming that the community's commitment and capacity to learn did reflect the board's proficiency to work in all three governance as leadership modes (i.e. fiduciary, strategic, and generative). All rural, public board chairpersons and presidents could point to several community projects or initiatives which would not have been possible without the direction and support of the college's strategic and operational plan.

An analysis of the documents and artifacts demonstrated the desire of a very effective board (IFIVE) to connect with their community, develop a vibrant learning community, and to move towards an integrated environment. Essentially, a very effective board values their community and sees the college as an integral part of innovation and the sustainability plan of the town, city, or region. Their planning documents reflect the provision of a strong college identity as a mature higher educational institution confidently meeting the diverse needs of the community learners. In contrast, the same analysis of a less effective board (ITWO) demonstrated a short-sightedness towards community commitment and capacity to learn, which was reflected in their business plan and policy development processes. Basically, a less effective board apparently sees the college's relationship with the community in a fundamental and practical sense and feels a sense of responsibility to appear to be open and co-operative to community programs and events.

Generally speaking, very effective boards, with guidance from their president and senior administration, appeared to stay current with community forces that may drive change. As well, they appeared to look backward and forward to understand what has emerged and conceptualize what may be possible.

CHAPTER 5

THE SUMMARY, CONCLUSIONS, AND
RECOMMENDATIONS

Summary

The purpose of this study was to explore the relationship between the practice of shared leadership and governance effectiveness within the nonprofit boards of the Western Canadian public and rural colleges. As well, given that such relationships do exist; do they make a difference in the performance of the college?

The study explored the linkages between two primary concepts – one about shared leadership and the other about governance effectiveness – within nonprofit governance. Oddly, shared leadership and governance effectiveness had not been linked previously, almost as if each concept was foreign to the other. Normally, nonprofit organizations have volunteer boards and institutional leaders. The former are expected to govern and the latter are expected to lead and manage. However, this study looked at the practice of shared leadership as a collaborative effort, between the board and the president, and other administrative staff, towards enriching the organization's perspective. As well, the study investigated governance effectiveness from the viewpoint of boards adding value – decisions and actions that may enhance the long-term quality, growth, and sustainability of the college – by the ways in which members work together.

Understanding that monitoring of performance is one of the responsibilities of governance, the study recognized that boards regularly examine the past, through a variety of data fields, to make sense of the alternatives for their college's desired state. Consequently, the study constructed quantitative explanations about the performance of colleges from the past three years of performance envelope results, as created by the Government of Alberta – Ministry of Advanced Education and Technology (2006). This evaluation requires all colleges to be assessed, and subsequently rewarded, on the basis of the following five key performance indicators: (1) student satisfaction, (2) employer satisfaction, (3) enrolment growth, (4) administrative expenses, and (5) enterprise revenue development. In closing, to reveal to what degree the factors of governance as leadership may contribute to institutional performance, the researcher intuited an objectivism approach, utilizing both positivism and constructivism perspectives.

Major Conclusions

The following are the major conclusions made from this thesis:

1. An Understanding of Shared Leadership is Foundational to Effectiveness

Dr. Robert Coles (2000) stated:

The truth is that; complain as we might about the absence of moral behavior in life today, we have to work to advance it.

We need to help one another along through the moral leadership we show, or through how we support it in others. (p. xii)

In today's world, all too often, governance has become a front-page story profiling negligent, unbridled, and acquiescent boards and presidents. As evidenced in this study, for moral leadership, or stewardship, to emerge, it is clear that nonprofit boards must first work on their understanding of governance as a collaborative effort. Generally, the colleges in the study recognized their own effectiveness as a function of adding value to the long-term growth and development of the college. As well, in seeking to understand the effects of today's situational realities – like globalization, urbanization, and regionalization – a board, in a rural setting, has a unique, and additional responsibility, that being, to serve the best interests of their community at large.

2. The Practicing of Shared Leadership Affects Competency Development

Draves and Coates (2007) argued that, "The attitudes, values, and behavior of the Industrial Age were good, but they are not appropriate for the Internet Age" (p.22). Normally, any complex system or organization will inevitably evolve in ways that no longer make sense when circumstances change. Hence, as seen in this study, adding value, and counteracting these rapid changes, college boards need to practice shared leadership, which is congruent with the development of new board competencies. These competencies, which once called for a fiduciary level participation, only, today require governance skills and abilities, such as working together at strategic and generative levels. This mission-critical shaping of shared leadership practices, as noted in the study, requires a base of shared values and an understanding of the roles and responsibilities of board members.

3. The College's Performance Reflects the Practicing of Shared Leadership

In relating performance to leadership, Garfield (1986) summarized:

> There is a special quality that leads to learned effectiveness and the results orientation of the peak performer. It, too, can be enhanced by training and distinguishes peak performers from ordinary performers. This special quality consists of an ability to take charge of one's work and its progress. To a significant degree, peak performers manage their own development (pp.138-139).

As profiled in this study, from a shared leadership perspective, learned effectiveness and a results orientation are at the heart of practicing governance, as opposed to doing governance. Also, the study demonstrated that constructing explanations about past performance, in concert with administration, is hard work for a college board, yet the practice can yield new strategies, innovations, or insights. Simply stated, taking the responsibility to manage their own development, is one of the first steps a college board can take towards capacity building for decision-making and influencing institutional performance. However, as the study noted, the journey can be stressful and awkward, at times, yet the rewards can be meaningful and enriching for the college's many learners.

4. The President's [Governance] Competency and Performance Can Positively Affect the Board's Effectiveness

In commenting on the impact of the president, Collins and Porras (2002) urged:

> We're asking you to think less in terms of being a brilliant (product) visionary or seeking the personality characteristics of charismatic leadership, and to think more in terms of being an organizational visionary and building the characteristics of a visionary (company) (p.41).

As noted in the study, when governors focus on institutional stewardship, their job becomes not so much about selecting the president, but rather the building of the policies and processes that will yield good presidents long after their term(s) has ended. As well, as shown in the study, an effective president seeks to build the college, in concert with the community and the board, by taking an architectural approach to organizational development. The building process begins by valuing and growing the role of nonprofit governance within the institution.

5. The Board's Human Capital Composition Can Positively Affect the Board's Effectiveness

Wishing to underscore the importance of trust to sustainable innovation, Friedman (2006) stated, "Indeed, the United States has become one of the great meeting points in the world, a place where lots of different people bond, learn to trust one another, and build myriad horizontal friendships and alliances" (p.320). Similarly, a high-trust board can become a 'great meeting point' where consensus is developed on a set of values, a vision, a mission, and outcomes. As seen in the study, these governance-related ends statements can reflect the institution's history and culture, and prove to be more enduring than the individual. As well, the statements can reflect the rich diversity of the membership of the board. Additionally, this study demonstrated that in a rural environment, which is impacted by globalization, urbanization, and regionalization, diversity in the composition of the board's membership capital becomes a synonymous factor with competitive advantage and learned effectiveness.

6. The Board's Governance-related Education and Training Can Positively Affect the Board's Effectiveness

Commenting on a specific board development strategy, Chait, Holland, and Taylor (1996) offered, "Despite the apprehensions of some, veteran board members and seasoned presidents almost always cite retreats as the single most powerful lever to direct attention to board effectiveness and to devise the means to strengthen board performance" (p.37). Normally, as evidenced in this study, a new board member's acceptance of the benefits of governance as a collective effort is not readily understood or linked to board effectiveness and performance. Prior to this acceptance occurring, there appeared to be a need to learn about their role and responsibilities as a board member. Similarly, it was noted that an understanding of an institution's challenges, programs, and priorities only become meaningful to a board member, if they can relate them to shared values, a common vision, and a set of key performance outcomes.

In short, faced with today's postsecondary education challenges –
globalization, urbanization, and regionalization – the study demonstrated the
need for rural board members to become governance experts as soon as
possible. However, in contrast, it was evident that some boards did not
consciously and systematically create opportunities to expand the
[governance] knowledge base of their boards. Nevertheless, as evidenced,
boards that participated in targeted, ongoing training did demonstrate
effectiveness, improved competency levels, and higher institutional
performance ratings.

7. **The Board's View of Themselves as Stewards and Listeners to the
   College's Voice is Fundamental to the Understanding of Governance
   Responsibility**

When reflecting on the institutionalization of dysfunctional [governance]
thinking, Gore (2006) stated:

> My reasoning here is simple: free men and women who feel
> individual responsibility for a particular part of the earth are, by
> and large, its most effective protectors, defenders, and
> stewards. Wherever this sense of responsibility is diluted or
> compromised by competing imperatives, the likelihood of
> stewardship and care for the environment diminishes (p.275).

As noted in the study, when a rural college in a sparsely populated
region is under ministerial pressure to demonstrate institutional performance,
the remote learners are vulnerable to the devolution of programs and services.
For example, when a senior administrator was provided with an annual bonus
based upon the size of the unreserved net asset base, the college was likely to
cut programs and services on the periphery of the rural college's catchment

area – or open an urban campus where direct costs of delivery may have been lower. Similarly, when a board acquiesced their governance role to a charismatic president, and chose to meet irregularly, then the politicians were loath to assert the learner's right to enhanced learning opportunities, services, and facilities.

Edgar Schein, in Senge, Scharmer, Jaworski, and Flowers (2004), said, "If you want to understand an organization's culture, go to a meeting" (p.48). He believed that we can always learn much more about organizational culture through careful observation and reflective participation than from reading mission or value statements. The disciplined application of Schein's insight to the board's value for and practice of listening to the college's voice, is found in their ability to temporarily suspend their own values, attitudes, and opinions. As evidenced in the study, they discover and build capacity to see the organization as a whole, thereby activating their imagination and creativity.

In summary, no other factor in the study – president's governance competency and performance, human capital composition of the board, and governance-related education and training – appeared to elicit such a collective endorsement from the rural boards. This stunning revelation may be implying a fundamental difference between governance in an urban setting and a rural, or non-metro, setting. Very often, we found that rural boards find themselves thinking and working together counteracting threats, fears and denial – fear of enrolment decline, the threat of take-over by an urban institution, and denial of the impacts of globalization, urbanization, and regionalization upon their college. Clearly, these defenders, protectors, and stewards need a new reality and a redirection of their energy towards hope and possibility that's grounded in ideas and experiences emerging from innovators in education, science, business, and their communities.

8. The Rural Community's Commitment and Capacity to Learn Reflects the College Board's Proficiency to Practice Governance as Leadership

In present day Western Canada, rich in natural resources, workers need more training and skill development than ever before as their employers deal with the same rate of change and turnover that are challenging the colleges. Zeiss (1997) pointed out that workforce development has the potential to transform the [comprehensive community] college into a different kind of learning organization – one that is deeply attuned to the needs of business, industry, and the broader community.

The study validated the fact that rural colleges, with boards who embrace strategic and generative planning, take their community capacity building and workforce development roles seriously, and are being recognized provincially in these areas. Ironically, when many college presidents and board chairs were asked about the size and service of their institutions, they typically reported only credit earning programs and students. Often, however, their continuing education and workforce development departments serve as many or more community learners each year. Yet, it is worthwhile to note that much of this activity is classified by the Ministry of Advanced Education and Technology as either non-credit in nature or peripheral to the mandate of the college. Nevertheless, community capacity building has emerged into the light and appears to be headed toward centre stage for its contribution to learning in the rural college.

Specific Conclusions

Given the current context, I see a fundamental barrier to the practice of shared leadership in board governance. Allow me to explain. Nonprofit boards in the college sector have the primary legal responsibility for governance. They reserve to themselves organizational oversight and policy making, and delegate to the president responsibility for managing the operations and resources. Very effective boards which practice shared leadership are not just outside examiners, but also powerful forces supporting the organization and its president.

However, while respecting this division of labour, it is essential for boards to become allies with their president in the pursuit of the values, vision, mission and outcomes. The practice of shared leadership is severely challenged when there is a lack of understanding by the board, or the president, that both parties are essential complementary ingredients to the governance partnership that, when combined, are greater than the sum of their parts. Whereas, very effective boards recognize that they cannot govern well without the president's collaboration and that the president cannot lead the institution to its full potential without the board's unflagging support; less effective boards find themselves in a precarious position, influenced by a confrontational relationship with their president, of attempting to shape the direction of the college and govern from a distance. Whereas, very effective boards tend to forge a partnership with the president, which is characterized by mutual trust, forthrightness, and a common

197

commitment to the vision and the outcomes; less effective boards, who are not open and honest with their president, struggle mightily in attempting to face and resolve problems early.

Very effective boards welcome differing points of view and strategic and generative thinking at the board table. Board members of very effective boards communicate regularly with the president, and members of senior administration, informally discussing concerns in and between board meetings. Hence, a very effective board governs in a constructive partnership with the president and the senior administrative team, recognizing that the effectiveness of the board and president are interdependent.

Consequently, as a result of this study, it is my opinion that there is a relationship between the practice of shared leadership and board effectiveness, and indeed, it can make a difference in a rural institution's performance. Given the challenges of globalization, urbanization, and regionalization, which are impacting non-metro colleges, I believe there is a need for consideration of a new approach or paradigm of nonprofit governance. However, such a new approach will require more dedication, discipline, and focus than is presently exhibited within conventional governance structures. If, as most board members agree, stewardship is central to the understanding and practicing of governance in the nonprofit sector then, by definition, governance as stewardship is at the apex of any board development model. Therefore, board members need to be carefully selected, be properly prepared, exhibit enthusiasm for the task at hand, work collectively, and commit to become protectors, defenders, and stewards of their college. Most board members will acknowledge these qualifications as the price of doing value-added work for their community and their college. Those that cannot acknowledge these covenants would be advised to consider other avocations.

The challenges that governance as stewardship will pose, for presidents and other senior administrators, are more about letting go of the need to assume the risk and the need to do the majority of the critical thinking. It is not the adding of additional responsibilities for strategic planning and accountabilities. Far too often, nonprofit boards mistake their engagement and effectiveness for a president-directed set of governance exercises which serve to shield the board from the real work of the college.

Allow me to stress that there is nothing wrong with conventional governance structures; however, boards in rural Western Canada need to face the fact that their situational realities are vastly different than their urban counterparts. In many cases, their institution, although much smaller than a similar urban institution, is the largest employer in the city, town, or region. Community development – social, recreational, cultural, and workforce – is perceived by the citizenry to be a primary responsibility of the local college in a rural setting. Seldom are urban institutions, because of their size and influence, threatened by public policy pronouncements, new envelop distributions of resources, or discussions at the ministerial level regarding the regionalization of the system.

In believing these facts to be substantiated and valid, the attainment of governance as stewardship represents an alternative approach to ensuring enhanced learning opportunities for Western Canadian students. The model, which I call the Stewardship Pyramid, defines governance as stewardship as a direct result of the incremental aggregation, development, and performance on a consistent basis of the mission critical duties of a board.

The diagram of the Pyramid that accompanies this explanation should be self-explanatory. However, I want to point out and emphasize a few of the important ideas, as I considered them, in constructing it.

Any structure must be built on a solid foundation and the cornerstones of the foundation are the most significant part of it. You will note that the cornerstones of this governance structure are an understanding of the roles and responsibilities and the articulation of the institution's vision and outcomes. Since these two components have been discussed at some length under other headings, I shall not repeat it here. The heart of the body is extremely important and, since architects have been known to stress the heart of buildings that they have created, I have selected three governance essentials – risk identification, policy development, and strategic planning – which comprise the heart of the structure. Catalytic boards that differentiate, do so as a function of being anticipatory, thus reducing unpredictability. They balance their planning with politics, and see policy development as their greatest legacy.

Further to my explanation, I should like to call attention to the top of the structure. The apex is governance as stewardship and it should be remembered that it is stewardship that widens the circle of opportunity for rural learners, deepens the meaning of life-long learning in a community, and strengthens the bonds of the colleges with their many partners. Furthermore, governance as stewardship is not easy to attain and the connecting points – accountability and power – to the apex are meant to indicate this. You must be continually accountable to your many publics and recognize that power (and influence) is a direct benefit of the public recognition achieved by demonstrating a more integrated college community of shared values and responsibilities.

Also, the connecting blocks, generative thinking and shared leadership, upon which governance as stewardship rests are vitally interwoven in the process of reaching the apex. Generative thinking and shared leadership both come from rural boards being prepared and are vital requisites for being an innovative and highly competitive institution. Those boards that lack generative thinking capacity are certain to be lacking in their commitment to shared leadership and will regress in their actions and behaviors when the stressful situations arise.

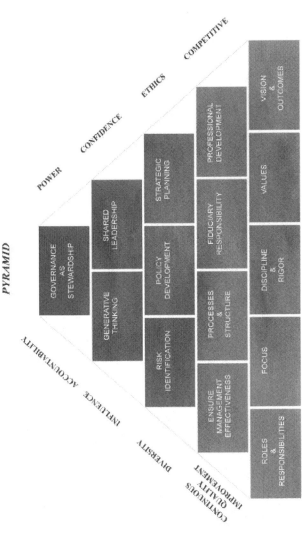

THE STEWARDSHIP PYRAMID

GOVERNANCE AS STEWARDSHIP is central to the governance system in the non-profit sector and is a direct result of the incremental aggregation, development, and performing of the mission critical duties of a board, on a consistent basis.

Figure 3.0

The Stewardship Pyramid – Governance as Stewardship

Specific Recommendations

Specific recommendations emanating from this study are noted to enhance the governance of the [rural] college boards. In short, the recommendations call for an immediate and thorough board governance review by the Ministry of Advanced Education and Technology.

Given that an effective, nonprofit board of governors should have a clear view of their role in relation to management and institutional performance; and, given that boards require some independence from government; and, given that the boards remain government organizations that should be effective, policy-based, accountable, and subject to direction and support; and, given that government recognizes that a robust college is a function of an effective, nonprofit board; it is recommended as follows:

1. The Minister(s) of Advanced Education and Technology develop an updated set of foundational principles, standards, and guidelines to ensure boards implement specific components of effective, nonprofit governance. These principles should serve the enhancement of policy development in the following areas: shared leadership, role and responsibilities, ends statements, relationship with the ministry, executive limitations, governance processes, board-staff relationships, accountability, transparency, ethics, professional development, selection and succession, and communications.

2. In concert with governing boards, the Minister(s) of Advanced Education and Technology review their performance envelope

framework and criteria, to ensure institutions are fairly and equitably rewarded for their efforts in aligning with ministerial and institution goals. In addition to the present criteria, the review should take into account institutional performance in the following new areas: collaborations, partnerships, community [economic and social] development, non-credit courses and programs, workforce development, and the building of vibrant learning communities.

3. In concert with governing boards, In concert with the governing boards, the Minister(s) of Advanced Education and Technology review and update public policy as it applies to board appointments, re-appointment, chairperson selection and appointment, human capital composition, nomination, advertisement and recruitment, size of the board, frequency of meetings, compensation, term(s), orientation, ongoing governance-related training, continuous quality improvement, risk management, and recognition.

4. The Minister(s) of Advanced Education and Technology review and update public policy as it applies to the committee structure of boards. It is recommended that the Minister consider the obligatory inclusion of the following standing committees: (1) audit, (2) human resources, 3) professional development, (4) ethics, (5) external relations, (6) institutional performance, (7) recruitment, and (8) policy review.

Future Study Recommendations

In rural and regional settings, there is much scope for further advancement of the concepts of shared leadership and board effectiveness. Some potential inquiries, which may focus on effectiveness, leadership, performance, and various relationships and effects are presented as follows:

1. Within a decentralized orientation, the relationship(s) between the Ministry(s) of Advanced Education and Technology and the institution's board of governors.

2. Within a board governance setting, the relationship(s) between the chairperson and the president, chairperson and vice-chairperson, board executive and president, and president and the board.

3. Within a regional context, the relationship(s) between the institution's board of governance and their primary external partners, such as the community, governmental, business, industry and donors.

4. Within a globalization and urbanization context(s), a study focusing on the rural-urban interface and exploring the relationship(s) between a rural and urban institution.

5. With a regional context, the relationship(s) between the boards of several rural institutions with dissimilar mandates, visions, and values.

6. The effect(s) of ill-discipline, distractive and dissolute behaviors and actions of board members on governance as stewardship; together

with the factors of generative thinking and working together, shared leadership, and institutional performance.

7. The affect(s) of an integration orientation and the development of vibrant learning communities on the college and community – both seeking to share values, responsibilities, and benefits.

8. The affect(s) of urbanization and regionalization, in a multi-board setting, on their ability(s) to accrue and develop the necessary infrastructure, program development, and governance structure.

REFERENCES

Alberta Advanced Education. (2006). A *Learning Alberta – Final Report of the Steering Committee*. Alberta advanced education cataloguing in publication data. Edmonton, Alberta

American Federation of Teachers. (2006). *Shared Governance in Colleges and Universities – A Statement by the Higher Education Program and Policy Council*. Retrieved May 15, 2006, from, http://www.aft.org/pubs-reports/higher_ed/shared_governance.pdf

Andringa, R.C. & Engstrom, T.W. (2002). *Nonprofit Board Answer Book – Practical Guide for Board Members and Chief Executives*. Washington, DC: BoardSource

Bachman, D., Elfrink, J. & Venzana, G. (1999). E-mail and snail mail face off in rematch. *Marketing Research, 11* (4), 11-15

Barnes and Noble. (2004). *Search – Leadership, Trustee, Trusteeship, and Governance*. Retrieved May 15, 2006, from, http://www.barnesandnoble.com/

Bennis, W. (1989). *On Becoming a Leader*. Reading, MA: Addison-Wesley Publishing

Block, P. (1993). *Stewardship. Choosing Service over Self-Interest*. San Francisco, CA: Berrett-Koehler

Bolman, L.G. & Deal, T.E. (1995). *Leading with Soul*. San Francisco, CA: Jossey-Bass Publishers

Bolman, L.G. & Deal, T.E. (1997). *Reframing Organizations*. San Francisco, CA: Jossey-Bass Publishers

Bugg, G. & Dallhoff, S. (2006). *National Study on Board Governance Practices in the Nonprofit and Voluntary Sector in Canada*. Retrieved July 19, 2007, from http://www.cvsrd.org/eng/board_governance/docs/national_study.PDF

Burns, J.M. (1978). *Leadership*. New York, NY: Harper & Row, Publishers

Calder, B. & Andrews, G. (1984). *Rider Pride – The Story of Canada's Best-Loved Football Team*. Saskatoon, SK: Western Producer Prairie Books

Canadian Association of University Teachers. (2004). *CAUT Policy on governance – Where We Have Been and Where We Should Go.* Retrieved June 26, 2006, from www.caut.ca/en/about/committees/dp_governancepastfuture.pdf

Canadian Council on Learning. (2006). *Introducing the Composite Learning Index – Putting Lifelong Learning on the Map.* Retrieved June 27, 2006, from www.ccl-cca.ca/cli

Carter, J., & Carter, M. (1997). *Reinventing your Board.* San Francisco, CA: Jossey-Bass

Carter, T.S. & Man, T.L.M. (2003). *Good Governance in Meeting the Duties of Directors of Charities and Not-for-Profits.* Retrieved on June 27, 2006, from http://www.axi.ca/tca/jul2003/guestarticle_2.shtml

Carver, J. (1997). *Boards That Make a Difference.* San Francisco, CA: Jossey-Bass

Carver, J. (1997). *Reinventing your Board.* San Francisco, CA: Jossey-Bass

Chait, R.P. (2005). *Governance Now Conference.* Governance as leadership pp presentation notes. Regina, SK

Chait, R.P., Holland, T.P., & Taylor, B.E. (1996). *Improving the Performance of Governing Boards.* Phoenix, AZ: The Oryx Press

Chait, R.P., Ryan, W.P. & Taylor, B.E. (2005). *Governance as Leadership-Reframing the Work of Nonprofit Boards.* Hoboken, NJ: John Wiley & Sons Inc.

Collins, J. & Porras, J.I. (2002). *Built to Last.* New York, NY: Harper Collins Publishers Inc.

Coles, R. (2000). *Lives of Moral Leadership.* New York, NY: Random House

Commission on National Investment in Higher Education (1998). *Straight Talk About College Costs and Prices.* Retrieved September 29, 2007, from http://www.ed.gov/about/bdscomm/list/hiedfutwre/reports/0809-draft.pdf

Council for Aid to Education. (1998). *Breaking the Social Contract: The Fiscal Crisis in Higher Education.* Rand Corporation. 3 Apr. 1998. Retrieved June 27, 2006, from http://www.rand.org/publications/CAE/CAE100/index.html>

Covey, S.R. (2004). *The 8th Habit – From Effectiveness to Greatness.* New York, NY: Free Press – A Division of Simon & Schuster, Inc.

Crosby, P. (1989). *Let's Talk Quality.* New York, NY: McGraw-Hill

Crotty, M. (2003). *The Foundations of Social Research.* London, UK: Sage Publications, Ltd.

CUPE National Research Branch. *Social Services: A Guide to Non profit Governance.* Retrieved July 26, 2007, from http://cupe.ca/updir/A_Guide_to_Nonprofit_Goverance.pdf

Davis G. (1997). Orientation and professional development of trustees. *New Directions for Community Colleges.* Retrieved July, 7, 2005, from http://search.epnet.com/login.aspx?direct=true&db=eric&an=EJ49468

Deming, W.E. (1986). *Out of Crisis.* Cambridge, MA: MIT Centre for Advanced Engineering Study

Draves, W.A., & Coates, J. (2007). *Nine Shift.* River Falls, WI: Learning Resources Network

Drucker, P.F. (1974). *Management: Tasks, Responsibilities, Practices.* New York, NY: Harper Collins

Eadie, D. (2006). "Making a Good Board Better." *School Administrator.* Retrieved July 26, 2007, from http://proquest.umi.com/pqdweb?did=1043001841&sid=2&Fmt=3&clientId=589 35&RQT

Faris, R. (2006). *The Rural North American Conference.* Purpose: Towards learning communities' pp presentation notes. Calgary, AB

Ferguson, M. (1980). *Untitled Presentation to the World Future Society* Toronto, ON, July, 1980.

Flaherty, T.B., Honeycutt, E.D., Jr., & Powers, D. (1998). Exploring text-based electronic mail surveys as means of primary data collection. *The 1998 Academy of Marketing Science National Conference proceedings,* 260-64.

Friedman, T.L. (2006). *The World is Flat.* New York, NY: Penguin Group

Futter, V., Cion, J.A., & Overton, G. W. ed. (2002). *Nonprofit Governance and Management.* USA: The American Bar Association and the American Society of Corporate Secretaries

Garfield, C. (1986). *Peak Performers – The New Heroes of American Business.* New York, NY: Avon Books

Garfield, T.K. (2004). Current governing board legal issues. *New Directions for Community Colleges, 4*(125). San Francisco, CA: Jossey-Bass, Wiley Periodicals, Inc.

Gill, M. (2001). "Governance Do's and Don'ts: Lessons from Case Studies on Twenty Canadian Nonprofits, Final Report." Institute on Governance

Gill, M. (2002). "Building Effective Approaches to Governance." *The Nonprofit Quarterly,* Retrieved July 10, 2007, from: http://www.tsne.org/print/313.html, 9:2

Glesne, C. (1999). *Becoming Qualitative Researchers: An Introduction.* San Francisco, CA: Addison Wesley Longman

Gore, A. (2006). *Earth in the Balance – Ecology and the Human Spirit.* New York, NY: Rodale, Inc.

Governance Matters. *Benchmarks for Effective Boards.* Retrieved July 26, 2007, from http://www.governancematters.org/index.cfm?organization_id=56&section_id=988 &page

Greenleaf, R.K. (1977). *Servant Leadership: A Journey into the Nature of Legitimate Power and Greatness.* Mahwah, NJ: Paulist Press

Gorard, S. (2001). *Quantitative Methods in Educational Research: The Role of Numbers Made Easy.* London, UK: Continuum

Government of Alberta. *Board Governance Review Discussion Paper.* Board Governance Review Task Force. May 2007

Hall, P.D. (2006). The new globalism: Reflecting on the sources of transnational identity. In S. Batliwala & D. Brown. (Ed.), *Transnational Society and Global Governance.* (p.67). Kumarian Press Online

Heberlein, T.A., & Baumgartner, R. (1978). Factors affecting response rates to mailed surveys: A quantitative analysis of the published literature. *American Sociological Review, 43,* 447-462

Hemann, P. (1999). Elevating the discourse of your board. *Association Management.* 1 (88)

Harvard Business Review. (2000). *Empowering the Board.* Boston, MA: Harvard Business School Press

Heberlein, T.A., & Baumgartner, R. (1978). Factors affecting response rates to mailed surveys: A quantitative analysis of the published literature. *American Sociological Review, 43,* 447-462

Hillman, J. (1996). *The Soul's Code: In Search of Character and Calling.* New York, NY: Random House

Houle, C.O. (1989). *Governing Boards: Their Nature and Nurture.* San Francisco, CA: Jossey-Bass

Idealist.org. "Approaches to the History of Nonprofits." *Making the Nonprofit Sector in the United States: A Reader – A Response to David Hammack's Message by Peter Dobkin Hall.* Retrieved July 10, 2007, from http://www.idealist.org/npofaq/01/06.html.

Internet Nonprofit Centre. "The Consent Agenda: A Tool for Improving Governance." *BoardSource.* Retrieved July 10, 2007, from http://www.boardsource.org/Spotlight.asp?ID=14.245.

Jean, B. (2004). *The Road to Successful Rural Community Development: Ten Winning Conditions.* Retrieved June 26, 2006, from nre.concordia.ca1_ftp2004/nre2_annual_reports/NRE2_Annual_Report_english.pdf

Johnson, N.L. (2003). The *John Wooden Pyramid of Success.* Los Angeles, CA: Cool Titles

Kahane, A. (2004). Solving tough problems – An open way of talking, listening, and creating new realities. San Francisco, CA: Berrett-Koehler Publishers, Inc.

Kiesler, S., & Sproull, L.S. (1986). Response effects in the electronic survey. *Public Opinion Quarterly, 50,* 402-413

Kilgour, D. (1999). *In Search of Good governance.* Notes for remarks by D. Kilgour, P.C., M.P., Edmonton Southeast, to the 1999 Laurentian Seminar on Parliament and the Challenge of Good Governance. Retrieved June 26, 2006, from http://www.david-kilgour.com/mp/governance.htm

Lakeland College. (2006). *2006-2010 Business Plan*

Lakeland College. (2007). *Board Policy Handbook.* (January 2007)

Lang, D.W. (2005). Working boards in tertiary education: Lessons from three case studies. *Canadian Society for the Study of Higher Education, 2* (25), 4

Lorsch, J.W. (2000). Empowering the board. In Harvard Business Review on Corporate Governance. Boston, MA: Harvard Business School Press

Mace, M. (1971). *Directors: Myth and Reality.* Cambridge, MA: Harvard Business School Press

McNamara, C. (1997). "Basic Overview of Nonprofit Organizations." *Field Guide to Leadership and Supervision.* Retrieved July 10, 2007, from http://www.managementhelp.org_thry/np_thry/np_intro.htm.

Moxley, R.S. (2000). *Leadership and Spirit.* San Francisco, CA: Jossey-Bass

Nemerowicz, G. & Rosi, E. (1997). *Education for Leadership and Social Responsibility.* London, U.K.: Falmer Press

National Governors Association. (2001). *Five Actions Governors can Take Now to Strengthen Higher Education Governance.* Influencing the future of higher education. Retrieved July, 7, 2005, from http://www.agb.org/content/pages/actnow2.html.

O'Callaghan, P. & Korbin, J. (2000). *The Workers' Compensation Board of British Columbia Board Governance Review Report and Recommendations.* Retrieved July 26, 2007, from http://www.worksafebc.org/publications/reports/ocallaghan_korbin_report/korbin.pdf

Oliver, C. (1999). *The Policy Governance Fieldbook.* San Francisco, CA: Jossey-Bass

Osborne, D. & Gaebler, T. (1992). *Reinventing Government.* New York, NY: Penguin Group

Panel on Accountability and Governance in the Voluntary Sector (February 1999). "Building on Strength: Improving Governance and Accountability in Canada's Voluntary Sector." Retrieved July 10, 2007, from http://www.vsr-trsb.net/pagvs/

Peters, T.J. (1997). *The Circle of Innovation.* New York, NY: Alfred A. Knopf.

Peters, T.J. & Waterman, R.H. (1982). *In Search of Excellence.* New York, NY: Harper & Row

Quinn, J.B. (1977). "Strategic Goals: Process and Politics." *Sloan Management Review.* Fall 1977, p. 26

Red Deer College. (2006). Building Communities Through Learning. *2006-2010 Business Plan*

Red Deer College. (2006). *Board of Governors Policy.* (October 2006)

Rossman, G.B. & Rallis, S.F. (1998). *Learning in the Field: An Introduction to Qualitative Research.* Thousand Oaks, CA: Sage Publications, Ltd.

Salamon, L.M., & Geller, S.L. "Nonprofit Governance and Accountability" *Communiqué No. 4.* Baltimore: The Johns Hopkins Center for Civil Society Studies, October 2005

Salmon, W.J. (2000). Crisis prevention: How to gear up your board. In *Harvard Business Review on Corporate Governance.* Boston, MA: Harvard Business School Press

Schein, E.H. (1993). How can organizations learn faster? The challenge of entering the green room. *Sloan Management Review, 34*(2), 85-92

Sefa Dei, G.J., Hall, B.L. & Rosenberg, D.G. (2002). *Indigenous Knowledges in Global Contexts.* Toronto, ON: University of Toronto Press, Inc.

Senge, P.M. (1990). *The Fifth Discipline – The Art and Practice of the Learning Organization.* New York, NY: Currency Doubleday

Senge, P.M., Scharmer, C.O., Jaworski, J. & Flowers, B.S. (2004). *Presence – An Exploration of Profound Change in People, Organizations, and Society.* New York, NY: Doubleday

Sheehan, K. (2001). E-mail survey response rates: A review. *Journal of Journalism and Communication University of Oregon.* Retrieved September 2nd, 2007, from http://jcmc.indiana.edu/vol6/issue2/sheehan.html

Silverman L., & Taliento, L. (2006). What business execs don't know – but should – about nonprofits. *Stanford Social Innovation Review.* Retrieved July 26, 2007, from http://www.ssireview.org/articles/entry/what_business_execs_dont_know_but_should_about_nonprofits/

Skinner, W. (1986). The productivity paradox. *Harvard Business Review,* 64 (55-59)

Smith, C. (2001). *Olds College Board Retreat.* pp presentation notes. Community College League of California. Olds, AB

Smith, P.M. (2006). *Are you a Graduate of the John Wayne School of Leadership?* Retrieved May 17, 2006, from, *http://www.opi-inc.com/shared_leadership.htm.*

Society of Corporate Secretaries & Governance Professionals & The National Center for Nonprofit Boards. *Governance for Nonprofits: From Little leagues to Universities.* Retrieved July 26, 2007, from http://www.governanceprofessionals.org/governnfp/board.shtml

Swann, D. (2006). *Private Member Statement: Industrial Development.* Retrieved June 26, 2006, from, file://T:\SYSTEM\Temporary Internet Files\OLKDB\DSanGovNeg2.htm

The Canadian Association e-zine. *Good Governance in Meeting the Duties of Directors of Charities and Nonprofits.* July 2003. Retrieved July 26, 2007, from http://www.axi.ca/tca/jul2003/guestarticle_2.shtml

The Johns Hopkins Centre for Civil Society Studies. (2005). *Listening Post Project.* Retrieved June 26, 2006, from http://www.jhu.edu/listeningpost/

The 1995 Canada Games Final Report. (1995). *The Best Games Ever.* ISBN 0-9699851-0-X

United Way of Canada. Board Development Website. Retrieved July 10, 2007, from http://www.boarddevelopment.org/.

Waide, P.J. (2002). Undertaking a self-assessment or strategic study. In V. Futter (Ed.), *Nonprofit Governance and Management.* (p. 39). Chicago, IL: American Bar Association

Welch, J. (2005). *Winning*. New York, NY: Harper Collins Publishers, Inc.

Wikipedia. "Face Validity." Retrieved September 16, 2007, from
http://en.wikipedia.org/wiki/Face_validity.

Wikipedia. "Nonprofit Organization." *Redirected from Nonprofit Organizations*. Retrieved
July 10, 2007, from *http://en.wikipedia.org/wiki/Nonprofit_organizations*.

Wood, M.M. ed. (1996). *Nonprofit Boards and Leadership – Cases on Governance,
Change, and Board-Staff Dynamics*. San Francisco, CA: Jossey-Bass

Zeiss, T. & Associates (1997). *Developing the World's Best Workforce: An Agenda for
America's Community Colleges*. Washington, DC: Community College Press

Zohar, D. (1997). *Rewiring the Corporate Brain*. San Francisco, CA: Jossey Bass

APPENDICES

Appendix I   Certification of Institutional Ethics Review

UNIVERSITY OF
CALGARY

CERTIFICATION OF INSTITUTIONAL ETHICS REVIEW

This is to certify that the Conjoint Faculties Research Ethics Board at the University of Calgary has examined the following research proposal and found the proposed research involving human subjects to be in accordance with University of Calgary Guidelines and the Tri-Council Policy Statement on *"Ethical Conduct in Research Using Human Subjects"*. This form and accompanying letter constitute the Certification of Institutional Ethics Review.

File no: **5167**
Applicant(s):   **Herbert J. Thompson**
Department: **Education, Faculty of**
                  An Exploration of the Relationship Between the Practice of
Project Title: **Shared Leadership and Board Effectiveness Within the Rural**
                  Boards of the Public Colleges of Alberta

Sponsor (if
applicable):

Restrictions:

This Certification is subject to the following conditions:

1. Approval is granted only for the project and purposes described in the application.
2. Any modifications to the authorized protocol must be submitted to the Chair, Conjoint Faculties Research Ethics Board for approval.
3. A progress report must be submitted 12 months from the date of this Certification, and should provide the expected completion date for the project.
4. Written notification must be sent to the Board when the project is complete or terminated.

Janice Dickin, Ph.D, LL.B,   MAR 2 3 2007
Chair   Date:
Conjoint Faculties Research Ethics Board

Distribution: (1) Applicant, (2) Supervisor (if applicable), (3) Chair, Department/Faculty Research Ethics Committee, (4) Sponsor, (5) Conjoint Faculties Research Ethics Board (6) Research Services.

2500 University Drive N.W., Calgary, Alberta, Canada T2N 1N4   •   www.ucalgary.ca

218

Appendix II. Consent Forms

 UNIVERSITY OF **CALGARY**

MEMO

CONJOINT FACULTIES RESEARCH ETHICS BOARD
c/o Research Services
Main Floor, Energy Resources Research Building
3512 - 33 Street N.W., Calgary, Alberta T2L 1Y7
Telephone: (403) 220-3782
Fax: (403) 289 0693
Email: bonnie.scherrer@ucalgary.ca
Friday, March 23, 2007

To: **Herbert J. Thompson**
Education, Faculty of

From: Dr. Janice P. Dickin, Chair
Conjoint Faculties Research Ethics Board (CFREB)

Re: **Certification of Institutional Ethics Review:** An Exploration of the Relationship Between the Practice of Shared Leadership and Board Effectiveness Within the Rural Boards of the Public Colleges of Alberta

The above named research protocol has been granted ethical approval by the Conjoint Faculties Research Ethics Board for the University of Calgary.

Enclosed are the original, and one copy, of a signed **Certification of Institutional Ethics Review**. Please make note of the conditions stated on the Certification. A copy has been sent to your supervisor as well as to the Chair of your Department/Faculty Research Ethics Committee. In the event the research is funded, you should notify the sponsor of the research and provide them with a copy for their records. The Conjoint Faculties Research Ethics Board will retain a copy of the clearance on your file.

Please note, an annual/progress/final report must be filed with the CFREB twelve months from the date on your ethics clearance. A form for this purpose has been created, and may be found on the "Ethics" website, http://www.ucalgary.ca/UofC/research/html/ethics/reports.html

In closing let me take this opportunity to wish you the best of luck in your research endeavor.

Sincerely,

Bonnie Scherrer
For:
Janice Dickin, Ph.D., LL.B., Faculty of Communication and Culture and
Chair, Conjoint Faculties Research Ethics Board

Enclosures(2)
cc: Chair, Department/Faculty Research Ethics Committee
    Supervisor: David Kirby

UNIVERSITY OF
CALGARY

Consent Form – Board Chair/President

Name of Researcher, Faculty, Department, Telephone & Email:

Herbert John (Tom) Thompson, Faculty of Education, Doctorate in Higher Education.
(403) 556-8301, tthompson@oldscollege.ca

Supervisor:

Dr. David Kirby
Title of Project:

An Exploration of the Relationship between the Practice of Shared Leadership and Board Effectiveness within the Rural Boards of the Public Colleges of Alberta

This consent form, a copy of which has been given to you, is only part of the process of informed consent. If you want more details about something mentioned here, or information not included here, you should feel free to ask. Please take the time to read this carefully and to understand any accompanying information.

The University of Calgary Conjoint Faculties Research Ethics Board has approved this research study.

Purpose of the Study:

The purpose of this study is to explore the relationship between the practice of shared leadership and board effectiveness within the boards of the Alberta public rural colleges. The study will seek to identify and interpret changes in the way a board thinks and works collectively due to four governance factors for improving board effectiveness: (1) president's competency and performance, (2) human capital of the board, (3) education and training of board members, and (4) stewardship and the college's voice. This inquiry will include describing the concept of shared leadership, defining and describing the four factors of improving board effectiveness and analyzing changes in the way boards think and work collectively through an analytical framework of specific behavior(s) theory, based upon the work of Chait, Holland, and Taylor (1996). The study's framework delineates six

220

competency sets inherent in effective boards. The goal of the study will be to identify board effectiveness patterns and themes, as a function of the practice of shared leadership, and that may assist in explaining the effects on institutional performance.

What Will I Be Asked To Do?

You are asked to participate in a one-hour semi-structured interview at your workplace site. This interview will be tape recorded and transcribed. Your participation is entirely voluntary and you may withdraw from the study at any time without penalty. Data collected up to the point of withdrawal from the interviewee will be retained and used as research. A copy of the final approved dissertation will be provided to the participating site.

What Type of Personal Information Will Be Collected?
Should you agree to participate, you will be asked to provide your age, gender and educational level. All participants will remain anonymous through use of pseudonyms.

The pseudonym I choose for myself is:

_____

Are there Risks or Benefits if I Participate?

There are no risks to participating in this research. The benefit will be through this study and your participation; a contribution will be made towards the research in shared leadership and board governance effectiveness.

What Happens to the Information I Provide?

Participation is completely voluntary, anonymous and confidential. Due to the small sample size, anonymity will be limited as participants may recognize colleagues' identities in report of the data. You are free to discontinue participation at any time during the study. Data collected from the interviewee will be retained and used as research up to the point of withdrawal. No one except me, as the researcher, and my supervisor will be allowed to see or hear any of the answers to the interview tape. Group information will be summarized for any presentation or publication of results. Individual quotes will be written under self-chosen pseudonyms to ensure anonymity. The transcribed interviews will be kept under lock and key in Olds College, Office of the President, only accessible to me, as the researcher, and my supervisor. The anonymous data will be stored for three years on a disk at which time it will be permanently erased. Within the context of this study, there will be no opportunity to review material attributed to you prior to its inclusion in the report.

Signatures

Your signature on this form indicates that you 1) understand to your satisfaction the information provided to you about your participation in this research project, and 2) agree to participate as a research subject.

Interviews will be audio-taped.

In no way does this waive your legal rights nor release the investigators, sponsors, or involved institutions from their legal and professional responsibilities. You are free to withdraw from this research project at any time. You should feel free to ask for clarification or new information throughout your participation.

Participant's Name: (please print)

_____

Participant's Signature _____ Date: _____

Researcher's Name: (please print) _____

Researcher's Signature: _____ Date: _____

Questions/Concerns

If you have any further questions or want clarification regarding this research and/or your participation, please contact:

H.J. (Tom) Thompson   Dr. David Kirby
Doctoral candidate   Doctoral supervisor
Faculty of Education   University of Manitoba
University of Calgary   (204) 474-8951
(403) 556-8301   dkirby@ms.umanitoba.ca
tthompson@oldscollege.ca

If you have any concerns about the way you have been treated a participant, please contact Bonnie Scherrer, Associate Director, Research Services Office, University of Calgary at (403) 220-3782; email bonnie.scherrer@ucalgary.ca

A copy of this consent form has been provided to you to keep for your records and reference. The researcher has kept a copy of the consent form, as well.

If you have any concerns about the way you've been treated as a participant, please contact Patricia Evans, Associate Director, Research Services Office, University of Calgary at (403) 220-3782; email plevans@ucalgary.ca

A copy of this consent form has been given to you to keep for your records and reference. The investigator has kept a copy of the consent form.

UNIVERSITY OF
CALGARY

Name of Researcher, Faculty, Department, Telephone & Email:

Herbert John (Tom) Thompson, Faculty of Education, Doctorate in Higher Education. (403) 556-8301, tthompson@oldscollege.ca

Supervisor:

Dr. David Kirby
Title of Project:

<u>An Exploration of the Relationship between the Practice of Shared Leadership and Board Effectiveness within the Rural Boards of the Public Colleges of Alberta</u>
This consent form, a copy of which has been given to you, is only part of the process of informed consent. If you want more details about something mentioned here, or information not included here, you should feel free to ask. Please take the time to read this carefully and to understand any accompanying information.

The University of Calgary Conjoint Faculties Research Ethics Board has approved this research study.

Purpose of the Study:

The purpose of this study is to explore the relationship between the practice of shared leadership and board effectiveness within the boards of the Alberta public rural colleges. The study will seek to identify and interpret changes in the way a board thinks and works collectively due to four governance factors for improving board effectiveness: (1) president's competency and performance, (2) human capital of the board, (3) education and training of board members, and (4) stewardship and the college's voice. This inquiry will include describing the concept of shared leadership, defining and describing the four factors of improving board effectiveness and analyzing changes in the way boards think and work collectively through an analytical framework of specific behavior(s) theory, based upon the work of Chait, Holland, and Taylor (1996). The study's framework delineates six competency sets inherent in effective boards. The goal of the study will be to identify board effectiveness patterns and themes, as a function of the practice of shared leadership, and that may assist in explaining the effects on institutional performance.

What Will I Be Asked To Do?

You are asked to participate by providing various governance-related and public documents such as policy manuals, board orientation packages, annual reports, business plans, and performance envelope awards. It is expected that you would gather, package, and forward these documents to the researcher via pre-paid courier. Your participation is entirely voluntary and you may withdraw from the study at any time without penalty. Data and artifacts collected up to the point of withdrawal from the participants will be retained and used as research. No-one except the researcher, my supervisor and the participant will be allowed to see any of the data and artifacts, which are collected and where possible, stored on a computer disk under lock and key in Olds College, Office of the President. Within the context of this study, there will be no opportunity to review material attributed to you prior to its inclusion in the report. A copy of the final approved dissertation will be provided to the participating site.

What Type of Personal Information Will Be Collected?

All participants will remain anonymous through use of pseudonyms.

The pseudonym I choose for myself is:

_____

Are there Risks or Benefits if I Participate?

There are no risks to participating in this research. The benefit will be through this study and your participation; a contribution will be made towards the research in shared leadership and board governance effectiveness.

What Happens to the Information I Provide?

Participation is completely voluntary, anonymous and confidential. Due to the small sample size, anonymity will be limited as participants may recognize colleagues' identities in report of the data. You are free to discontinue participation at any time during the study. Data collected up to the point of withdrawal will be retained and used as research up to the point of withdrawal. No one except me, as the researcher, and my supervisor will be allowed to see the data. Information will be summarized for any presentation or publication of results. All data will be kept under lock and key in Olds College, Office of the President, only accessible to me, as the researcher, and my supervisor. The anonymous data will be stored for three years on a disk at which time it will be permanently erased. Within the context of this study, there will be no opportunity to review material attributed to you prior to its inclusion in the report.

Signatures

Your signature on this form indicates that you 1) understand to your satisfaction the information provided to you about your participation in this research project, and 2) agree to participate as a research subject.
In no way does this waive your legal rights nor release the investigators, sponsors, or involved institutions from their legal and professional responsibilities. You are free to withdraw from this research project at any time. You should feel free to ask for clarification or new information throughout your participation.

Participant's Name: (please print)

_____

Participant's Signature _____ Date: _____

Researcher's Name: (please print)

_____

Researcher's Signature: _____ Date: _____

Questions/Concerns

If you have any further questions or want clarification regarding this research and/or your participation, please contact:

H. J. (Tom) Thompson   Dr. David Kirby
Doctoral candidate   Doctoral supervisor
Faculty of Education   University of Manitoba
University of Calgary   (204) 474-8951
(403) 556-8301   dkirby@ms.umanitoba.ca
tthompson@oldscollege.ca

If you have any concerns about the way you have been treated as a participant, please contact Bonnie Scherrer, Associate Director, Research Services Office, University of Calgary at (403) 220-3782; email bonnie.scherrer@ucalgary.ca

A copy of this consent form has been provided to you to keep for your records and reference. The researcher has kept a copy of the consent form, as well.

If you have any concerns about the way you've been treated as a participant, please contact Patricia Evans, Associate Director, Research Services Office, University of Calgary at (403) 220-3782; email plevans@ucalgary.ca

A copy of this consent form has been given to you to keep for your records and reference. The investigator has kept a copy of the consent form.

Consent Form – On-Line Survey Questionnaire Board Member

Name of Researcher, Faculty, Department, Telephone & Email:

Herbert John (Tom) Thompson, Faculty of Education, Doctorate in Higher Education.
(403) 556-8301, tthompson@oldscollege.ca

Supervisor:

Dr. David Kirby

Title of Project:

An Exploration of the Relationship between the Practice of Shared Leadership and Board Effectiveness within the Rural Boards of the Public Colleges of Alberta

This consent form, a copy of which has been given to you, is only part of the process of informed consent. If you want more details about something mentioned here, or information not included here, you should feel free to ask. Please take the time to read this carefully and to understand any accompanying information.

The University of Calgary Conjoint Faculties Research Ethics Board has approved this research study.

Purpose of the Study:

The purpose of this study is to explore the relationship between the practice of shared leadership and board effectiveness within the boards of the Alberta public rural

228

colleges. The study will seek to identify and interpret changes in the way a board thinks and works collectively due to four governance factors for improving board effectiveness: (1) president's competency and performance, (2) human capital of the board, (3) education and training of board members, and (4) stewardship and the college's voice. This inquiry will include describing the concept of shared leadership, defining and describing the four factors of improving board effectiveness and analyzing changes in the way boards think and work collectively through an analytical framework of specific behavior(s) theory, based upon the work of Chait, Holland, and Taylor (1996). The study's framework delineates six competency sets inherent in effective boards. The goal of the study will be to identify board effectiveness patterns and themes, as a function of the practice of shared leadership, and that may assist in explaining the effects on institutional performance.

What Will I Be Asked To Do?

You are asked to participate by completing an on-line survey questionnaire, which will be in the form of a word document and forwarded to you as an attachment via e-mail at your workplace site. It is expected that you would return the completed survey questionnaire within 14 days of receipt. Your participation is entirely voluntary and you may withdraw from the study at any time without penalty. Data collected up to the point of withdrawal from the respondents will be retained and used as research. The anonymous data will be stored on a computer disk under lock and key in Olds College, Office of the President, accessible only to this researcher and my supervisor. A copy of the final approved dissertation will be provided to the participating site.

What Type of Personal Information Will Be Collected?

Should you agree to participate, you will be asked to provide your age, gender and educational level.

All participants will remain anonymous through use of pseudonyms.

The pseudonym I choose for myself is: _____

Are there Risks or Benefits if I Participate?

There are no risks to participating in this research. The benefit will be through this study and your participation; a contribution will be made towards the research in shared leadership and board governance effectiveness,

What Happens to the Information I Provide?

Participation is completely voluntary, anonymous and confidential. Due to the small sample size, anonymity will be limited as participants may recognize colleagues' identities in report of the data. You are free to discontinue participation at any time during the study. Survey questionnaire data collected from the respondents will be retained and used as research up to the point of withdrawal. No one except me, as the researcher, and my supervisor will be allowed to see the data. Group information will be summarized for any presentation or publication of results. The anonymous survey questionnaire data will be stored on a computer disk under lock and key in Olds College, Office of the President, accessible only to this researcher, and my supervisor. The anonymous data will be stored for three years on a disk at which time it will be permanently erased. Within the context of this study, there will be no opportunity to review the material attributed to you prior to its inclusion in the report.

Signatures:

Your signature on this form indicates that you 1) understand to your satisfaction the information provided to you about your participation in this research project, and 2) agree to participate as a research subject.

In no way does this waive your legal rights nor release the investigators, sponsors, or involved institutions from their legal and professional responsibilities. You are free to withdraw from this research project at any time. You should feel free to ask for clarification or new information throughout your participation.

Participant's Name: (please print)_____

Participant's Signature _____ Date:_____

Researcher's Name: (please print) _____

Researcher's Signature: _____ Date: _____

Questions/Concerns

If you have any further questions or want clarification regarding this research and/or your participation, please contact:

H.J. (Tom) Thompson	Dr. David Kirby
Doctoral Candidate	Doctoral supervisor
Faculty of Education	University of Manitoba
University of Calgary	(204) 474-8951

(403) 556-8301
dkirby@ms.umanitoba.ca tthompson@oldscollege.ca

If you have any concerns about the way you have been treated a participant, please contact Bonnie Scherrer, Associate Director, Research Services Office, University of Calgary at (403) 220-3782; email bonnie.scherrer@ucalgary.ca

A copy of this consent form has been provided to you to keep for your records and reference. The researcher has kept a copy of the consent form, as well.

Appendix III. Semi-structured Interview Questions

 UNIVERSITY OF
CALGARY

Interview Questions for college Presidents and board Chairpersons:

Introduction

The following research questions will be used to guide the investigation and information will be sought both through documentation analysis, semi-structured interviews, and survey questionnaires.

As noted in the researcher's proposal, the interviews will be used to encourage college Presidents and board Chairpersons to discuss their views regarding to what extent does their board practice shared leadership, what is the extent of the four factors, as identified in the literature, as being essential for board effectiveness, to what extent does the institution's performance reflect the board's practice of shared leadership, and to what extent does the larger community's higher education awareness, participation, and attainment reflect the board's practice of shared leadership.

Note: As well, it is noted in the researcher's proposal that the survey questionnaire will be sequenced to follow the completion of the semi-structured interviews, such that the survey questionnaire design may be informed by the interviews.

Definition of Terms used within the Interview Questions

1. Shared leadership – It is the collaborative governance act of developing, in concert with administration, the institution's values, vision, mission, outcomes, the determination of the preferred future state, and the assurance of the necessary resources to achieve the same.
2. Institutional performance – It is measured by five components, which are annually assessed by the Ministry of Advanced Education and rewarded within the context of the performance envelope: (i) strategic and ongoing enrolment growth, (ii) efficient

financial management and performance, (iii) demonstrated enterprise revenue development, (iv) student satisfaction, and (v) employer satisfaction.

3. Human capital – In the context of a board's composition, it is essentially the collective human resource contributions which board members bring to their governance experience. For example, human capital contributions could include such criteria as social, intellectual, economic, political, geographic, etc.

4. Stewardship – The representation of the interests of the owners and the act of approaching the college with respect and a sincere ability to listen to its voice.

5. Board governance effectiveness – Thinking and working collectively and in a consistent manner towards a focus on purposing, engaging, and enriching the board's governance process.

6. *Governance as leadership* modes – There are three modes of thinking and working together as a board: i) fiduciary – concerned primarily with the stewardship of the tangible assets, ii) strategic – create a strategic partnership with senior administration, and iii) generative – provide a less recognized but critical source of transformational leadership for the organization.

Questions

- Selecting one or two criteria from the following list comment upon the extent of understanding exhibited by your board relative to the practice of shared leadership.

    - focus on policy development and institutional performance?
    - provide of proactive and visionary leadership?
    - focus externally?
    - shape institutional direction?
    - assure the mission is achieved?
    - understand the complexity of issues?
    - demonstrate cohesiveness in seeking multiple perspectives?
    - ensure continuous learning?

- Selecting one or two criteria from the following list comment upon the extent to which your board practices shared leadership.

    - identified by the quality of the board members interactions rather than their positions?
    - evaluated by how board members think and work together rather than the problem(s) is solved by the leader?

233

- identified by the board's ability to enhance the [problem solving] process rather than provide the solution and answers?
- evaluated by the independence of all board members and their ability to be active in the leadership process rather than defer to distinct differences between leaders and followers?
- identified by communication which is conversational rather than formal?
- evaluated by the value for democratic processes, honesty, and shared ethics, which seeks a common good rather than secrecy, deception, and politics?

- Selecting one or two criteria from the following list comment upon the extent that the institution's performance reflects your board's practice of shared leadership.

  - employment rate of graduates?
  - graduate satisfaction?
  - incremental enrolment growth using a three-year rolling average?
  - administrative expenses as a percentage of overall college expenses?
  - enterprise revenue generation?

- What is the extent of the contribution of the president's [governance] competency and performance associated with the board's practice of shared leadership and board governance efficiency?

- What is the extent of the contribution of the board's human capital composition associated with their practice of shared leadership and board governance efficiency?

- What is the extent of the contribution of the board's governance-related education and training associated with their practice of shared leadership and board governance efficiency?

- What is the extent of the contribution of the board's view of themselves as stewards and listen to the college's voice associated with their practice of shared leadership and board governance efficiency?

- Are there one or two examples in your environment that would illustrate the external community's commitment and capacity to embrace life-long learning, which would reflect the extent to which your board works in all three *governance as leadership* modes?

Appendix IV.   Survey Questionnaire

Research Protocol: An Exploration of the Relationship Between the Practice of Shared Leadership and Board Effectiveness Within the Rural Boards of the Public Colleges of Alberta

The Board Assessment Survey Questionnaire

A. Introduction

The purpose of this study and related research protocol is to explore the relationship between the practice of shared leadership and board effectiveness within the boards of the Alberta public rural colleges. In order to achieve this purpose, the inquiry will seek to identify and interpret changes in the way a board thinks and works collectively due to four governance factors, as suggested by the literature, for improving board effectiveness: (1) the president's competency and performance as it relates to the development of a shared leadership governance model, (2) the human capital composition and mix of the board, (3) the evidence of systematic and targeted education and training in policy governance, and (4) the demonstration of stewardship and listening to the college's voice.

This examination will include describing the concept of shared leadership, defining and describing the four factors of improving board effectiveness and analyzing changes in the way boards think and work collectively through an analytical framework of specific behavior(s) theory, based upon the work of Chait et al (1996) – a framework of which delineates six competency sets inherent theoretically in effective boards. The goal of this study will be to identify board effectiveness patterns and themes, as a function of the practice of shared leadership, which may assist in explaining the associated effects on institutional performance.

B. Context

Understanding that no post secondary institution or individual will be named in the study, there are eight rural Alberta public colleges involved in this inquiry. The

236

study will include the following institutions: (1) Lakeland College, (2) Portage College, (3) Keyano College, (4) Grande Prairie Regional College, (5) Medicine Hat College, (6) Lethbridge College, (7) Red Deer College, and (8) Northern Lakes College.

The research process will involve a variety of investigative approaches gathering information from semi-structured interviews, the survey questionnaire, historical documentation, government documents and reports, business-related documents and college websites. The study will include interviews with board chairpersons and college presidents of the designated institutions, and in addition, **the on-line board assessment survey questionnaire has 37 questions and will hopefully be completed by all the board members of the eight participating colleges.**

C. Request for Co-operation

You are requested to participate by completing the on-line board assessment survey questionnaire, which follows. It is anticipated that you would return your completed survey questionnaire within 14 days of receipt to the following e-mail address: tthompson@oldscollege.ca

Your participation is valued and is entirely voluntary. You may withdraw from the study at any time without penalty. Data collected up to the point of withdrawal from you will be retained and used as research. The anonymous data will be stored for three years on a computer disk under lock and key in Olds College, Office of the President, accessible only to this researcher and my supervisor. Within the context of this study, there will be no opportunity to review the responses attributed to you prior to its inclusion in the report. A copy of the final approved dissertation will be provided to the participating college.

There are no risks to participating in the survey questionnaire portion of the research. The benefit will be through this study and your participation; a contribution will be made towards the research in shared leadership and board governance effectiveness.

D. Personal Information

Should you agree to participate, in the spaces provided please provide the following information:

Age ___ Gender ___ Education Level _____ Occupation _____

All participants will remain anonymous through the use of pseudonyms. In the space provided, please choose a pseudonym name for yourself.

_____

E. Questions and/or Concerns

Should you have further questions or want clarification regarding this research and/or our participation, please contact:

H.J. (Tom) Thompson, Doctoral Candidate, tthompson@oldscollege.ca, (403) 556-8301

Or

Dr. David Kirby, Doctoral Supervisor, dkirby@ms.umanitoba.ca, (204) 474-8951

F. Definition of Terms

1. Shared leadership – the collaborative governance act of developing, in concert with administration, the college's values, vision, mission, the determination of the preferred future state, and the assurance of the necessary resources to achieve the same.

2. Institutional performance – is measured by five components, which are generally assessed annually by the Ministry of Advanced Education. As a consequence of the assessment colleges are rewarded financially within the context of the performance envelope, which measures five criteria. They are as follows: (i) strategic and ongoing enrolment growth, (ii) efficient financial management and performance, (iii) demonstrated enterprise revenue development, (iv) student satisfaction, and (v) employer satisfaction.

3. Human capital – is the collective human resource characteristics and contributions which board members bring to their policy governance experience. For example, human capital characteristics may include such criteria as social, intellectual, economic, political, geographic, etc.

4. Board governance effectiveness – is the act of thinking and working together in an ongoing and consistent manner, while applying their focus towards purposing, engaging, and enriching the board's governance capacity and shared leadership processes.

5. Shared leadership modes – are the three modes of thinking and working together as a board. They are as follows: (i) fiduciary – focused primarily with the stewardship of the college's tangible assets, (ii) strategic – focused on the creation of long range planning and high level strategic directions and initiatives, and (iii) generative – focused on becoming the source of transformational leadership for the college.

G. The Board Assessment Survey Questions

1. *Shared leadership understanding* – please respond by answering yes or no to the following questions. You are requested to place an "x" within the parenthesis of your chosen response.

a. Yes ( ) No ( ) Your board focuses on policy development and institutional performance.

b. Yes ( ) No ( ) Your board provides proactive and visionary leadership in concert with senior administration.

c. Yes ( ) No ( ) Your board focuses externally.

d. Yes ( ) No ( ) Your board shapes institutional direction in concert with senior administration.

e. Yes ( ) No ( ) Your board assures the College's vision is monitored and achieved.

f. Yes ( ) No ( ) Your board understands the complexity of the issues it faces.

g. Yes ( ) No ( ) Your board demonstrates cohesiveness in seeking multiple perspectives to a challenge.

h. Yes ( ) No ( ) Your board values continuous learning.

2. *Practicing shared leadership* – please respond by answering yes or no to the following questions. You are requested to place an "x" within the parenthesis of your chosen response.

a. Yes ( ) No ( ) Your board's interactions are identified by their alignment with organizational values and board policies rather than by their positions on issues.

b. Yes ( ) No ( ) Your board is characterized by how you think and work together rather than by problems being solved exclusively by the leader(s).

c. Yes ( ) No ( ) Your board is identified by their ability to enhance the problem solving process rather than the provision of solutions and answers.

d. Yes ( ) No ( ) Your board is characterized by their ability to be active collectively in the leadership process rather than to defer to distinct differences between perceived leaders and followers.

e. Yes ( ) No ( ) Your board is identified by their interpersonal communication which is conversational rather than formal.

f. Yes ( ) No ( ) Your board demonstrates their value on a consistent basis for stewardship, democratic processes, honesty, and shared ethics.

g. Yes ( ) No ( ) Your board *out governs* the competition.

h. Yes ( ) No ( ) Your board performs skillfully in all three modes of thinking and working together – i.e. fiduciary, strategic and generative.

3. *Focus on institutional performance* – from the choices provided please respond by placing an "x" in the space provided next to your preferred response.

a. Your board focuses on the employment rate of graduates.

( ) (i) every board meeting

( ) (ii) once every 3-4 months

( ) (iii) never

( ) (iv) once a year

b. Your board focuses on the satisfaction of graduates.

( ) (i) every board meeting

( ) (ii) once every 3-4 months

( ) (iii) never

( ) (iv) once a year

c. Your board focuses on sustainable enrolment growth.

( ) (i) every board meeting

( ) (ii) once every 3-4 months

( ) (iii) never

( ) (iv) once a year

d. Your board focuses on administrative expenses as percentage of overall college expenses.

( ) (i) every board meeting

( ) (ii) once every 3-4 months

( ) (iii) never

( ) (iv) once a year

e. Your board focuses on the creation of enterprise-related revenue streams.

( ) (i) every board meeting

( ) (ii) once every 3-4 months

( ) (iii) never

( ) (iv) once a year

4. *President's governance-related knowledge, skills, and abilities associated with the board's practice of shared leadership and board governance efficiency* – from the choices provided please respond by placing an "x" in the space provided next to your preferred response.

    a. The President engages your board and senior administration in strategic planning.

      ( ) (i) every board meeting

      ( ) (ii) once every 3-4 months

      ( ) (iii) not very often

      ( ) (iv) once a year during the approval process associated with the business plan

    b. The President works with the board and senior administration towards the development of a common vision for the college.

      ( ) (i) every board meeting

      ( ) (ii) once every 3-4 months

      ( ) (iii) not very often

( ) (iv) once a year during a workshop or retreat

c. The President works well with the board chairperson to provide
    good meeting management.

    ( ) (i) every board meeting

    ( ) (ii) once every 3-4 months

    ( ) (iii) not very often

d. The President works well with the board members and senior
    administration in proposing and managing change.

    ( ) (i) every board meeting

    ( ) (ii) once every 3-4 months

    ( ) (iii) not very often

    ( ) (iv) once a year during the approval process associated with
    annual budget

e. The President works with the board members and senior
    administration in maintaining low levels of internal conflict at the
    board table.

    ( ) (i) every board meeting

    ( ) (ii) once every 3-4 months

    ( ) (iii) not very often

5. *The Board's competencies which underscore board governance efficiency* –
please respond by answering yes or no to the following questions. You are
requested to place an "x" within the parenthesis of your chosen response.

    a. Yes ( ) No ( ) Your board understands [listens] and takes into
account the culture and norms of the college it governs.

    b. Yes ( ) No ( ) Your board takes the necessary [education and
training] steps to ensure that all members are knowledgeable about
the college, the profession, and the board's roles, responsibilities,
and performance.

    c. Yes ( ) No ( ) Your board nurtures the [professional]
development of all members as a working group, attends to the
board's collective welfare, and fosters a sense of cohesiveness.

    d. Yes ( ) No ( ) Your board recognizes the complexities and
subtleties of issues and accepts ambiguity and uncertainty as
healthy preconditions for critical discussion.

    e. Yes ( ) No ( ) Your board accepts as a primary responsibility the
need to develop and maintain healthy relationships among major
constituencies and stakeholders.

    f. Yes ( ) No ( ) Your board helps the college envision a direction
and shape a strategy.

6. *The Board's human capital* – please respond by placing an "x" within the
parenthesis if the following elements of human capital presently exist and
are utilized within the composition and mix of your board.

    a. Yes ( ) No ( ) Intellectual capital – i.e. individual board members
do technical work.

245

b. Yes ( ) No ( ) Reputational capital – i.e. college leverages the
board members political and corporate influence.

c. Yes ( ) No ( ) Political capital – i.e. an external heavyweight or
more: e.g. board members exercise power on the outside.

d. Yes ( ) No ( ) Social capital – i.e. board members strengthen
relationships to gain personal advantage.

e. Yes ( ) No ( ) Logic capital – i.e. the presence of logical,
practical, intuitive, or pragmatic dynamic(s) associated with the
board members decision making process(s).

7. *In conclusion, using one example from the college's external environment,
please comment illustrating how the community' commitment to life-long
learning [or not] may be a reflection of your board's governance-related
work.*

_____

_____

_____

_____

_____

Thank you

246

Made in the USA
San Bernardino, CA
22 December 2017